Marguerite Duras and Charles Bukowski:

The Yin and Yang of Modern Erotic Literature

Scott Shaw

Buddha Rose Publications

The text was originally composed as part of the
requirements for the Masters of Arts degree in
Humanities awarded by California State University,
Dominguez Hills.

First Edition 2007
First Hardcover Edition 2020

ISBN: 1-949251-26-8
ISBN-13: 978-1-949251-26-5

Library of Congress Control Number: 2009932283

10 9 8 7 6 5 4 3 2 1
Printed in the United States of America

Table of Contents

Introduction

Marguerite Duras and Charles Bukowski were born in vastly different parts of the world near the beginning of the twentieth century. Duras was born in French Indochina and Bukowski was born in Germany. Though the cultural surroundings where these two authors began their lives were elementally different, they both came to define their writing styles from events that took place in their early lives.

As a late adolescent, Duras, following her French heritage, left Indochina and relocated to France; post her having a love affair with an older Chinese man. This affair, and the literature which was born from it, would later come to be one of the central elements that would define Duras as a respected literary figure. Bukowski was brought from Germany to his father's native Los Angeles, California where, as a young boy, he found himself taunted as an outsider, thus, setting the stage for him to develop as the alienated writer of modern literature he was later to become.

Duras and Bukowski, in their early years, shared the experience of being identified as something other than the societal norm. This emotion of being deemed outsiders came to be the formulative element that came define the lives and the literature of Marguerite Duras and Charles Bukowski.

When studying the literature of Marguerite Duras and Charles Bukowski, it is clear that they each embraced a unique individual literary style that not only penetratingly depicted life experiences but also did so from the perspective of unique personal knowledge. It is commonly understood that an author draws upon his own experience when creating his literary works. Most authors, however, are reluctant to bring their own life into the acute autobiographical focus, as was the case with Duras and Bukowski.

Marguerite Duras, in her writings, detailed the life experiences of herself and her characters from a highly defined female perspective. Duras wrote with the trenchant understanding of a woman who not only draws on her own life experiences when creating her literature but studies and clearly defines the emotions that delineate the rational and irrational decision of her characters, as well.

Charles Bukowski was an admitted chronic alcoholic, womanizer, and horse race track enthusiast. His writings focused on his own alienation from society, his attempts to find a monetary means of survival, and his torrid love affairs with women. Whereas, Duras looks deeply into her characters, Bukowski's disaffection for society keeps his literature on the surface, depicting a new level of male dominant drunken bohemianism.

Marguerite Duras and Charles Bukowski, in their literature, each presented unique autobiographical voices: female and male respectively. From these voices one often finds their literature delving in the realms of the erotic: Duras from a female perspective and Bukowski from a blatantly male standpoint. In addition, they each focused upon and depicted a unique segment of twentieth century culture from their own specific points of view.

In this work we will see that both Marguerite Duras and Charles Bukowski were each dramatically shaped by their early life experiences, established in the environment of a dysfunctional family. From their early negative exposure and emotional indoctrination to life, Duras and Bukowski each developed as individuals who, at a young age, acted out behavior that was in direct conflict with the commonly accepted standard of their individual societal norms. From the moment these authors made the adolescent choices that they did, the rest of their physical and emotional existence was ultimately defined. What was created was a body of literary work that truly came to shape modern erotic literature.

Marguerite Duras

Marguerite Duras was born Marguerite Donnadieu on 4 April 1914 in Gia Ding, French Indochina. Gia Dinh is a suburb of Saigon, in modern day Vietnam.

Marguerite Duras' father was Henri Donnadieu, a mathematician by training. He was from the *Lot-et-Garonne* region of Southwestern France. He was lured to Indochina by the French propaganda of promised fortune in this seemingly exotic location. Thus, he relocated his new wife and two sons from a previous marriage to Southeast Asia. Duras' mother, Marie Legrand, was an elementary school teacher from the *Pas-de-Calais* area of Northern France.

In 1918, when Duras was three years old, the family moved from Gia Dinh to Phnom Phen. This move came about due to her father's appointment to a teaching position in this city. Her father soon became ill with an infectious fever and returned to France. The family remained in Indochina. Alain Vircondelet states in the biography he authored, *Duras,*

> *Marie Donnadieu doesn't go with him, as if fastened to this land of Indochina, a prisoner of her mission. She remains alone with the children.*

With her mother's choosing to remain in Phnom Phen, the fate of the Donnadieu family, and that of the literature created at the hand of Marguerite Duras, was set into motion.

It was soon after he returned to France that Duras' father died, leaving the family financially challenged. Her mother, due to her grief at the death of her husband, her impending poverty, and the trials of raising her daughter and her two step sons alone, faded into a functional insanity—a psychological state often referenced by Duras in her autobiographically based novels.

> *The mother is afraid of the surrounding yard, of the murmuring density of the vegetation, of prowlers, of the native servants whom she never completely trusts; she has the children sleep in her bed.*

The remaining family eventually left Phnom Phen and first moved to Song Co Chien, then Sadec, onto Vinh Long, and finally to Cholon, a suburb of Saigon, where Duras' mother maintained the family by following her profession as a school teacher. Except for the occasional trip to France, Duras' childhood and adolescence unfolded in this geographic location.

Marguerite Donnadieu, during her adolescence, changed her name to Marguerite Duras. The name, "Duras," was the name of a village in the *Lot-et-Garonne* area of France where her father was born.

At the age of nineteen, Duras left Indochina for France to study law at the *Faculte' de droit* and political science at the *Ecole libre des sciences politiques*. In 1935 she obtained her law degree and a diploma in political science.

Marguerite Duras began writing short stories during her late adolescence. It was in 1943, at the age of twenty-five, when her first novel, *Les*

9

Impudents, was published. Her second novel, *La Vie Tranquille,* was published a year later. From the mid 1940's forward, Marguerite Duras was a widely published author of novels and short stories, in addition to being a playwright, a screenwriter, and the director of nineteen of the films that she wrote. As her literary career progressed, Duras emerged as one of the leading figures in the reformation of modern literature. The structureless style of storyline, in which she composed her later writings, helped to redefine the boundaries of modern literature.

Central to the theme of all Duras' literature is that of a woman's perception of love, violence, being at odds against society, and the intimate detailing of erotic knowledge that she lifts to a new level of artistic vision. Anne Callahan, in her essay, *Vagabondage Duras,* states,

> *Duras makes enormous advances towards a new moment in the writing of erotic love in literature: when feminist artists, by developing alternative narrative strategies, can write about women's pleasure without shame. Duras writes primarily for women like herself, women whose erotic imagination has been nurtured in and by the pleasure of reading fiction. Duras, herself, has written for our pleasure some of the most seductive feminine texts, telling stories of sexual bliss at a privileged moment of total submission to a pleasure of the flesh which in its most extreme form we would call bondage.*

Duras bases her storylines in desire: desire for a specific outcome or a desire for things to be different than they are—a desire that inevitably never comes to pass.

Duras' literary characters, whether they are first person autobiographical or third person, are continually guided towards a set of predestined circumstances that they have little ability to control. Once the characters find themselves engulfed in these occurrences, their personal desire for fulfillment takes hold of them. They then struggle against overwhelming odds to maintain the level of intoxication that was present at the outset of these unexpected circumstances. Any early euphoria experienced by her characters is, however, never again embraced. As Trista Selous states in her book, *The Other Woman,*

> *Her texts constantly restage problems of sexual desire, its relation to identity and to death, and they invite the reader to fantasize the desires of the figures portrayed.*

With desire as a basis for all emotions, Duras' literature delves deeply into the affected areas of the protagonist's body and mind. Whether the desires are driven by love, lust, or a passion for power, this emotion is what leads her characters down a path to ultimately becoming ostracized by the other central characters or society as a whole.

Carol J. Murphy, in her essay, *Duras' L'Amant: Memories from an Absent Photo,* writes,

> *Duras' works are replete with frustrated narrators who avow the futility of*

11

recapturing the past while simultaneously and obsessively reliving the past.

These factors of desirous obsession, unfulfilled dreams, and lack of personal power and control drive the characters in Duras' novels. The central characters never truly find peace and are left, at best, moving on to a new mental or geographic location where new desires may be implanted.

Duras bases much of her literary work on personal interactions and memories. These memories often times involve factors and occurrences that took place during her childhood and the period when she was a young adult. At this period of time, Duras found herself in various locations in Asia. Thus, she used Asia as a backdrop for several of her works of literature.

Duras commonly leads her characters down a path of obsession, in one form or another. With a particular obsessive desire being their motivation, Duras' characters are continually driven to step beyond the levels of accepted behavior and push the boundaries of culture, love, and elemental life understandings, as Duras herself did in her own adolescence.

Ultimately, Duras bases much of her literature in the obsessive behavior she herself experienced and understood. From this, not only did Duras write some of the most compelling novels of the twentieth century, but also she was instrumental in expanding the range of technique in which a storyline was allowed to unfold.

Each of Duras' progressive literary works possesses a different quality and a variance of style. Therefore, one cannot view her work in an overall, uniform fashion. Instead, her novels must be viewed individually in order to see how her understanding of literature progresses, raising her to the level of master of her craft. For this reason, we will view the style and technique of individual novels composed by Duras. From this method of examination, we can hope to come to a precise understanding of the formation and execution of the Duras style of eroticism.

During Duras' adolescence, in Indochina, she came into contact with a Chinese man with whom she became infatuated. This meeting ultimately led to her having her first sexual experience. As is often the case, the first sexual experience is a most memorable factor in the life of a young girl. As Duras has based entire novels on this experience, it was obviously a defining factor in her life. Though she has penned novels which deal with other subjects and other loves, this first encounter seems to have permeated her consciousness and has given rise to her ability to acutely detail experiences in terms of the erotic. For this reason, we will first view the three novels where Duras describes the events that lead up to and ultimately culminated in her first sexual encounter; they are *The Sea Wall, The Lover,* and *The North China Lover.*

The Sea Wall was first published in France in 1950 as, *Un Barrage Contre Le Pacifique.* This was Duras' third published novel. Her first novel, *Les Impudents,* which has since been withdrawn, at the request of the author, and her second novel, *La Vie Tranquille,* was never translated into English.

As *The Sea Wall* was one of Duras' early published works, it reflects more the opening path she took in defining her literary style as opposed to representing what may be deemed the mature Duras style of literature. *The Sea Wall* is written in traditional novelistic fashion. The story takes a predominately linear course, and there is little that can be viewed as remarkable in this novel when comparing it to the truly inspired later works of Duras.

When comparing *The Sea Wall* to the later autobiographically based works of Duras, this novel is not revolutionary in its literary application. The style of the work can be defined as a product of the time, as it is similar in narrative story structure to other novels, especially those composed by American writers, during the mid twentieth century.

Alfred Cimaru, in his text, *Marguerite Duras,* confirms this fact by detailing the criticism presented by Germaine Bree. He writes,

> *This piece of dialogue, whose tone is duplicated throughout Un Barrage contre le Pacifique, reveals the growing influence of the American-type novel on Marguerite Duras. 'Un Barrage contre le Pacifique, Germaine Bree stated, was a story in the manner of the American novel, a la Hemingway.'*

The Sea Wall tells the story of Duras' family inching their way towards a gradually deepening physical and emotional poverty in Indochina. The character name that Duras uses to depict herself in this novel is Suzanne.

The styling of *The Sea Wall* is reminiscent of narrative Hemingway, in the sense that each setting and attributing factor of the storyline is acutely described. An example of this literary detailing can be observed in the passage,

> *Suzanne and Joseph had always known that phonograph. It had been bought by their father a year before his death and Ma had never separated herself from it.*

In addition to an acutely described environment, each attribute of the various characters is equally precisely depicted. This is especially the case of Duras' character, Suzanne.

Trista Selous in her study on Duras, *The Other Woman,* claims,

> *In Un barrage contre le Pacific and Le Petits Cheveaux de Tarquinia, Duras shifts to third person narration, with the result that the reader is distanced to varying degrees from all the figures, since the text is constructed as being produced from somewhere 'beyond' the events narrated. However, in each of these novels free indirect speech is used in relation to one figure, Suzanne and Sara respectively, so that the reader/narratee appears to have privileged insight into their thoughts, and is offered identification with them, although that identification is always somewhat uncertain, since free indirect speech produces an ambiguity around the question of who exactly is speaking.*

Much of what is described in this novel induces a state of sympathy directed in particular towards the Suzanne character and her mother. This

15

was, no doubt, an intentional act on the part of Duras. Alfred Cismaru states in his text, *Marguerite Duras,*

> *Solitude and boredom are ills constantly decried by the followers of the New School, and Marguerite Duras does not fail to share in similar apprehensions. The horse dies, of course, almost as soon as it is purchased. And whatever other escapes the personages thinks of, vanish sooner or later: the diamond has to be sold; the money received for it disappears into the pocks of creditors; need of further funds makes the sale of the phonograph imperative. In the case of Suzanne, company is so painfully absent that she has no recourse but to sit by the road, waiting; But no car stopped in front of the bungalow.*

As Duras actually lived much of what is written in this novel, her sympathetic depictions of occurrences can be viewed as her psychologically grieving for her childhood, when she was set at odds against the world, through no fault of her own. From her precisely writing about the details of her young life, Duras perhaps frees herself, to some degree, from the obvious pain she felt during this period of her life.

The Chinese man with whom Duras has her first sexual encounter is named Monsieur Jo in this novel. Whereas, her later novels dealing with this man and their love affair; namely, *The Lover* and *The North China Lover,* are driven by their lustful relationship, *The Sea Wall* is not. Instead, this novel is defined by the family's poverty, due to the death of Suzanne's father, and her mother's attempt to raise the family out of this destitution by giving piano lessons and being a pianist at *the Eden Cinema,* where she is described as having worked under horrible conditions for ten years to support the family.

Sexuality is referenced in *The Sea Wall,* yet it is not elementally formative to this work. Thus, this novel cannot truly be seen as a work based in eroticism. The subtle texture in which Duras writes of erotic elements can, none-the-less, be cited to gain a frame of reference for the inception of where Duras' erotic literature began.

> *Her mouth was red, the same red as her fingernails. It did something to me to see them together, so close. As if she had hurt her fingers and her mouth and it was her blood I was seeing, a little of the inside of her body.*

From this simple and profound depiction of lips and fingernails one can see how the subtle abstract literary styling of Duras sets the stage for her to continue the storyline on further, leading towards the eventual act of love and love making.

Another sentence that deserves study, to come to a more precise understanding of the this period of her life, is,

> *The wind blew her dress against her and I could see the shape of her breasts almost as if she was naked.*

From this sentence, the previous passage, and similar subtle erotic descriptions, the reader is allowed to savor the precise portrayal of what is taking place and is drawn deeply into the storyline. This is accomplished by acutely describing a situation. With this, Duras lures the reader into the subtle realms of the erotic, while not presenting them in an overwhelming manner.

It is evident how Duras, even at this early period of her writing career, had the ability to view situations not only from her own perspective, but to critically delve into the mind of the other characters of her novel; not only describing them, but allowing the reader to experience a small portion of what they may have been feeling, as well. This area of literary expertise is perhaps the best example of how early Duras literature was able to subtly draw upon the erotic without delving into the implied sexual situations in an overt manner.

When one views Duras' descriptions of carnal activity in *The Sea Wall*, it is immediately clear that she uses her acute sensory perception in the telling of the story.

> *When night had come, Monsieur Jo had drawn near Suzanne and had put his arm around her. The car continued to roll through the chaotic brilliance and darkness of the city. And Monsieur Jo's hand trembled. Suzanne could not see his face. Almost with out knowing it, he had pressed her close to him, and Suzanne allowed it. She was intoxicated with the city. The car drove onward, the only reality, a glorious reality. And in its wake all the city fell back, crumbled away, brilliant, swarming, alive, and endless. Sometimes Monsieur Jo's hand touched Suzanne's breasts. And once he*

said: "Your breasts are beautiful," The
thing had been said very softly. But it had
been said. For the first time. And while the
naked hand was on the naked breast. And
above the terrifying city, Suzanne saw her
breasts, saw the erection of her breasts
higher than anything that stood up in the
city. Her breasts they would be justified.

From this paragraph one can come to realize that early on in her literary career Duras possessed an understanding for masterfully isolating and depicting direct sexual activities, without becoming lost in the act of sexuality itself. The reader is told how the young girl's breasts are being fondled. Yet, the young girl's attention is not solely on the activity that is taking place. Instead, her mind goes to the city that surrounds her. This technique of storytelling shows how Duras allows herself to witness situations in her writing, portraying more than simply one activity and never becoming totally lost in the realm of the physical.

With this literary technique, the reader is led through the novel, never being forced to solely focus on the sexuality that is ongoing. Instead, the reader is continually guided away from the sexually obvious, thus, making the specifically erotic parts of the book less important then the emotions of the characters that make up this novel. This is Duras' greatest achievement in *The Sea Wall,* the ability to describe the erotic without making it acutely necessary to the storyline.

Duras' novel, *The Lover,* was written between May and February, 1984 and first published in French as *L'Amant.* This novel is no doubt the culminating masterpiece of Duras' career in eroticism. The work is so simply worded that the reader is led along the storyline almost as if reading common prose instead of a novel. The lack of unnecessary wording is what makes this novel such a masterpiece. As so often is the case, a novelist will elaborately describe and then redescribe a situation or event in order that the reader may be drawn into the storyline. Duras, on the other hand, uses such simple, yet explanatory wording, that the need for unnecessary depictions is alleviated.

Xaviere Gauthier in her interview with Duras, which was published under the title, *Woman to Woman,* explores the way in which Duras uses language in her style of literature. Duras states,

> *I'm never concerned about the sense or the meaning. If there's sense, it shows up afterwards.*

This simple statement is an ideal utterance that can be use in defining the mature work of Duras. Duras' mature style is devoid of the literary tradition of linear narrative.

Not all literary critics find the non-linear literary style that Duras presented in The Lover universally acceptable, however. Trista Selous, for example, in her text, *The Other Woman,* states,

> *...there is no absolute point of view from which the story is being told and which can either be accepted or criticized. Secondly, the interest lies not so much in the answer to questions posed in the text, but rather in the generation of the question, much of which requires a lot of sympathetic imagination on*

the part of the reader, as opposed to intellectual analysis.

The Lover is written in a stark autobiographical style. The story of her life and more particularly that of her first experiences of love in French Indochina are written in an opaque, stream of consciousness styling. The reader is instantly drawn into the emotional soul of the writer, Duras, as the term "I" is commonly intermingled with a secondary description of her life experience; it is as if some other entity, a second persona outside of herself is witnessing what is occurring in her life. This multiple observation styling is combined with a continual shifting of the timeframe—from the moment the experience occurs, onto reflections about what took place in retrospect; and then finally onto remembrances of other time periods in her life.

In the 1986 short story entitled, *La Pute de la cote normande,* Duras defines her understanding of her composition of this novel, comparing it to the literary structure in which she composed her earlier novel on the same subject, *The Sea Wall.* She writes,

> *In The Sea Wall I denied that passion of mine for love itself and I, as a narrator, wasn't present. Instead The Lover is me, I'm always present there, me and not my mother, not my brothers, not the Chinese lover. The heart of The Sea Wall, which is a political novel, is the capitalist world. The heart of The Lover is myself. I am the heart and all the rest of the book, because there's no literature there: only writing.*

Marilyn R. Schuster in her work *Marguerite Duras Revisited* refers to fact of Duras' continual retelling of the same tale in different novels and by various literary structures. She writes,

> *Many of Duras' works are retold tales. Although it could be argued that all storytelling is a reworking of other tales, in Duras' work the retelling itself is a central concern.*

In *The Lover,* Duras gives herself the ability to reflect and describe the experiences that she has taken mental note of, experiences that have led her onto the understanding she possessed at the time of writing this novel, many years after the time it was lived. For example, Duras reflects on and remembers a photograph of her son,

> *I found a photograph of my son when he was twenty. He's in California with his friends, Erika and Elizabeth Lennard. He's thin, so thin you'd think he was a white Ugandan too. His smile strikes me as arrogant, derisive. He's trying to assume the warped image of a young drifter. That's how he likes to see himself, poor, with that poor boy's look, that attitude of someone young and thin.*

After describing this very personal and seemingly critical analysis of a memory of a photograph of her son, she immediately ties this apparently unrelated statement into the storyline by finishing it with the claim,

It's this photograph that comes closest to the one never taken of the girl (herself) on the ferry.

Here we see how in this book, there is a constant intermingling of autobiographical, remembering, "I," immediately associated with a non-involved secondary personage viewing the young Duras' rite of passage and coming into her own definition of accepted social interaction. This type of literary shifting is constant throughout the book. Charles Krance, writes in his essay, *Dura(s) Space (some musings and reflections on reading/seeing Duras),*

> *For Duras, Being itself becomes apocryphal, a parasitic parody of non-being. A mock-heroic pun on the coexistence of space and time as a unified idea and experience.*

Verena Andermatt Conley in her essay *Duras and the Scene of Writing* describes the literary style of *The Lover.* She writes,

> *L'Amant is written from that ordinary scene of a past, the beginning of which has never really been present. Everything is dislocated, in dislocation: The French girl in Indochina, the Chinese lover in Saigon ostracized both by the girl's family and his own; the girl in relation to her own family; she lives in a boarding house, a pension, not a home.*

23

In *The Lover,* Duras possessed the ability to vividly remember and then depict her emotions at fifteen. She would do this while shifting from third to first person literary styles. For example,

> *She says I'd rather you didn't love me. But if you do, I'd like you to as you usually do with women.*

This shifting styling continually draws the reader deeper into the narration of the tale of this young girl. *The Lover* begins in the narrative by stating,

> *One day, I was already old, in the entrance of a public place a man came up to me. He introduced himself and said, "I've known you for years. Everyone says you were beautiful when you were young, but I want to tell you I think you're more beautiful now than then. Rather than your face as a young woman, I prefer your face now as it is, Ravaged."*

As if answering her own question to the universal inquiry of time and aging, Duras begins this book not with an excuse but with a description of how time takes its toll on all of us. From this passage, the reader is allowed to immediately understand how this is a tale of remembrance, not one of initial experience.

From time, one is allowed to gain perspective and refine knowledge from experiences that have occurred in the past. Duras allows herself this reflection, within this novel; not making excuses for time elapsed, instead, depicting that she is still alive, functional, and is still attractive, though time has aged her.

Duras continues on in the early pages of *The Lover* by reflecting further on time and aging by stating,

> *Very early in my life it was too late. It was already too late when I was eighteen. Between eighteen and twenty-five my face took off in a new direction. I grew old at eighteen. I don't know if it's the same for everyone, I've never asked. But I believe I've heard of the way time can suddenly accelerate on people when they're going through even the most youthful and highly esteemed stages of life. My aging was very sudden. I saw it spread over my features one by one, changing the relationship between them, making the eyes larger, the expression sadder, the mouth more final, leaving great creases in the forehead. But instead of being dismayed I watched the process with the same sort of interest I might have taken in the reading of a book.*

This ongoing descriptive process of aging, in the early part of *The Lover*, is definitive to the style in which this book is written. This is because it gives reason and definition for Duras' continual timeframe shifts. Without these early reflections and description of the body she now inhabits, the various time remembrances would possess no storyline validity.

Duras' writing, throughout *The Lover*, though apparently fragmented, is continually brought back into perspective as the ongoing tale of a young girl's first love is told. In fact, the random structural elements comprising this nonlinear storyline add to the depiction of Duras' philosophic observations of life.

Marilyn R. Schuster in her essay, *"Durasophiles" and "Durasophobes,"* sites the study on Duras by Sharon Willis, who attempts to detail Duras' techniques in the nonlinear format. Schuster paraphrases,

> *Sharon Willis in her study on Marguerite Duras: Writings on the Body, suggests that Duras produces emphatic and contradictory readings because she transgresses conventions, undermines expectations, and places uncomfortable demands on the reader: 'In their invariable display that something is missing, her fictions are about expectations unfulfilled. Perhaps it is this potential for deception and withholding that makes her fiction alluring. This is not a passive disappointment, for Duras' force lies in her Active subversion of expectation and demand.'*

Throughout *The Lover* Duras utilizes random subplots to describe the mindset of her character as an adolescent. In each subplot the factors that dominate her character's emotions are presented in a very precise manner. The various subplots all lead to the conclusion that throughout her life Duras obviously possessed a sense of not belonging, of being different, and of possessing a strong sense of insecurity. This fact is brought into clear focus as she describes herself as a child.

It's not the shoes though that make the girl look so strangely, so weirdly dressed. No. it's the fact that she's wearing a man's flat-brimmed hat, a brownish-pink fedora with a broad black ribbon. The crucial ambiguity of the image lies in the hat. How I came by it I've forgotten. I can't think who could have given it to me. It must have been my mother who bought it for me. I asked her. The one thing certain is that it was another markdown, another final reduction. But why was it bought? No woman, no girl wore a man's fedora in the colony then. No native, either.

The fedora she details is central to the description of this young Caucasian girl in Indochina. She refers to her wearing of it as if it is almost a badge of her difference from the society around her: both Colonial and Asian.

Duras goes on in *The Lover* describing her adolescent insecurity. On the day she first encounters the wealthy Chinese man with whom she falls in love with, she writes,

On the ferry, look I've still got my hair. Fifteen and a half. I'm using make-up already. I use Creme Tokalon, and try to camouflage the freckles on my cheeks, under the eyes. On top of the Crème Tokalon I put natural--color powder—Houbigant. Inside the limousine there's a very elegant man looking at me. He's not a white man. He's wearing European clothes—the light tussore suit of the Saigon Bankers. He's looking at me. I'm used to people looking at me.

27

People look at white women in the colonies;
at twelve-year-old white girls too. For the
past three years white men too, have been
looking at me in the streets, and my
mother's men friends have been kindly
asking me to have tea with them then while
their wives are out playing tennis at the
Sporting Club.
I could get it wrong, could think I'm
beautiful like women who really are
beautiful, like women who are looked at, just
because people really do look at me a lot. I
know it's not a question of beauty, though,
but of something else, for example, yes,
something else—mind, for example.

In addition to insecurity, Marguerite Duras throughout *The Lover* details the dysfunctional factors of her family. In references to her mother, she continually paints her in a less than affectionate manner and alludes to the fact of her impending insanity due to the pains of poverty and Duras' troublesome older brother. Duras writes,

In the books I've written about my childhood
I can't remember, suddenly, what I left out,
what I said. I think I wrote about our love
for our mother, but I don't know if I wrote
about how we hated her too...

From the previous passage we can come to understand that Duras' relationship with her mother was psychologically complicated. Duras obviously possessed life long unresolved feelings about her mother. At one moment the lady would be represented as a being deserving sympathy, damned by the constraints of destiny, in the next, her shortcoming would be acutely detailed. As Anne Callahan states in her essay, *Vagabondage: Duras,*

> *...Marguerite's mother send her on a channel crossing which is to be her rite of passage into the world of desire. The beautiful seductive child is dressed to kill. She is wearing a pure silk dress, almost transparent, her mother's dress. This dress is sleeveless, very low cut. Her mother gave it to her because it was too light for the mother to wear.*

Throughout *The Lover,* Duras attempts to detail that she, in fact, had control over her young life's path and her choice to become the lover of an older Chinese man. She was, in fact, dominated by the set of circumstances that were presented to her at an early age by her mother and her brothers. This is not unusual. Duras, however, though claiming the power of choice, continually returns, throughout her literary career, to detailing the family orientated factors that led up to the youthful choices she made. Thus, she could not psychologically separate her definitive actions of that year from the emotional influences of her mother and brothers.

Much of the dysfunctional stimuli of Duras' family in *The Lover* and the other two novels directly written about this particular period of time are attributed to her oldest brother. She possessed obvious distaste for him, as he continued a lifelong path of opium addiction, violence, and a general disregard for human life.

In *The Lover* it is detailed that he once attempted to molest the family housekeeper. In other Duras works it is told that he actually consummated the act.

One cannot help but wonder whether Duras, herself, was molested by her oldest brother at a young age. If she was, it can be understood why she did not directly reference this fact in her literature and instead attributed the act of first love to her Chinese lover. She, none-the-less, continually referred to her oldest brother in the most negative manner in all of her works where he is mentioned.

In addition to the possibility of molestation, Duras held her older brother directly responsible for the death of her other brother, to whom she was much closer. It is described that he was killed in Indochina in December 1942, during Japanese occupation. Duras writes,

> *Not only do we never have any celebrations in our family, not a Christmas tree, or so much as an embroidered handkerchief or a flower. We don't even take notice of death, any funeral, any remembrance. There's just her. My elder brother will always be a murderer. My younger brother will die because of him. As for me, I left, tore myself away.*

Obviously, as is documented in her literature, emotional abuse occurred at the hands of her oldest brother towards herself, her second brother, and her mother. If sexual abuse did occurred towards Duras, it sheds light on the fact of why Duras detailed intermittent love and distaste for her mother. As is often times the case, if a child is molested by a direct family member it is natural for her to, at least in part, blame the parent for possessing a lack of control to stop the molestation from occurring. Thus, this may explain much of Duras' varying emotions in her autobiographical literature towards her mother.

From a literary perspective, the emotions Duras depicts in her writings about her mother are varied. Yet, in an autobiographical essay, written in 1987, three years after she composed *The Lover,* Duras writes in a much more affectionate manner about her mother. She states,

> *What to say? I will speak of her, of the mother. The mother in Whole Days in the Trees, and the one in The Sea Wall, is the same. Ours. Yours. Mine, as well. The one I loved was French. She was a woman from the north of France. A daughter of Flemish farmers, of those endless wheat fields, of northern Europe. She would be a hundred years old now (she had her last child when she was near forty). Good student. Scholarship student—like me, later on—she had studied education. At twenty-five, she went to Indochina—it must have been between 1905 and 1910. And there, in the villages of the bush, she taught French and arithmetic to the little Annamites. In that era piracy was prevalent in Indochina, as were leprosy, hunger, and cholera.*
>
> *Nothing stopped Mother, she spoke of her youth over there as a period of happiness. Then she was married and three children followed. When I think about her now, it's under her maiden name that I see her: Marie Legrand.*

This paradox between literary subject matter and true emotional feelings is constant through the life and the literature of Marguerite Duras. In fact, it is virtually impossible to define which of her statements are true and which are composed solely for the reason of creating startling literary material. This fact is expanded upon by Marilyn R. Schuster in her text, *Marguerite Duras Revisited.* In it she writes,

> *Although there is an abundance of material about her life, it is difficult to know the woman. Duras has said repeatedly that dates and the kinds of facts biographers seek to verify are of no concern to her. What matters is the story of the unconsciousness, of what lives beneath the surface of the 'objective' data. For many events in her life, however, especially concerning her childhood in Indochina, she is the only remaining witness. No two 'chronologies' of her life given in biographies interviews, or special issues of literary magazines are exactly alike.*

With this understanding as a basis, Duras was allowed to use the artistic license she found desirable to compose her stories, as autobiographical as they may have been, to form the perspective most appropriate to describe the factors she wished the reader to focus upon.

Duras, in *The Lover,* artistically tells the tale of a family in chaos. All of these detailed stories delving into the psyche of Duras' family take the reader deeper into the mind of Duras, herself, and the factors that supposedly led to the choices she made in her young life; the choices that ultimately guided her to the eroticism portrayed in this novel, with the older Chinese man.

Her family naturally possessed reservations about her love affair with an older Asian man. But, as is so often the case with the adolescent mindset, Duras' character used this as motivation to jump deeply into her love affair with this man, shunning her family's dissatisfaction and using it as a reason to move forward with the relationship.

As the tale unfolds in *The Lover,* it can be surmised that though Duras believed she was worthy of the Chinese man's affections, predominately due to her age and her Caucasian heritage, she did not possess a great sense of self worth. Statements such as,

> *Every morning the little slut goes to have her body caressed by a filthy Chinese millionaire.*

clearly depict this. Though this statement is obviously what Duras expected others to be thinking about her, it, none-the-less, reflects her state of mind as not only being separated and different by her choice to be with this man, but additionally, it peers into her own consciousness as a person and the baggage she took with her throughout her life.

The erotic sexuality of *The Lover* is very blatant. Duras writes,

> *I tell him to come over to me, tell him he must possess me again. He comes over. He smells pleasantly of English cigarettes, expensive, perfume, honey, his skin has*

taken on the scent of silk, the fruity smell of silk tussore, the smell of gold, he's desirable. I tell him of this desire. He tells me to wait awhile. Talks to me, says he knew right away, when we were crossing the river, that I'd be like this after my first lover, that I'd love love, he says he knows now I'll deceive him and deceive all men I'm ever with. He says as for him he's been the cause of his own unhappiness. I'm pleased with all he's foretold, and he says so. He becomes rough, desperate, he throws himself on me, devours the childish breasts, shouts insults. I close my eyes on the intense pleasure. I think, He's used to it, this is his occupation in life, love, nothing else. His hands are expert, marvelous, perfect. I'm very lucky, obviously, it's as if it were his profession, as if unwittingly he knew exactly what to do and what to say. He calls me a whore, a slut, he says I'm his only love, and that's what he ought to say, and what you do say when you just let things say themselves, when you let the body alone, to seek and find what it takes what it likes, and then everything is right, and nothing's wasted, the waste is covered over and all is swept away in the torrent, in the force of desire.

What one can come to learn of Duras' eroticism from the preceding paragraph is, not only did she enjoy embellishing herself as a woman who would eventually control and manipulate men but that the sense and ideology of sex being somehow wrong permeated her mind as it is continually

34

associated with such terminology as "Whore" and "Slut."

Duras ends *The Lover* with a discussion of the fact of how she met up with her lover years later in Paris. She states,

> *Years after the war, after marriages, children, divorces, books, he came to Paris with his wife. He phoned her. It's me. She recognized him at once from the voice.*
> *He said, I just wanted to hear your voice. She said, It's me, hello. He was nervous, afraid, as before. His voice suddenly trembled. And with the trembling, suddenly, she heard the voice of China. He knew she'd begun writing books, he'd heard about it through her mother whom he'd met in Saigon. And about her younger brother, and he'd been grieved for her. Then he didn't know what to say. And then he told her.*
> *Told her that it was as before, that he still loved her, he could never stop loving her, that he'd love her until death.*

The literary impact of this final paragraph is one of the most effective elements in this novel. Duras, throughout this book, has set the stage for the reader to become intimately enthralled with her character's rite of passage. This conversation brings the entire story to a dramatic climax. As to whether or not it did or did not, in fact, take place, is almost unimportant. The fact that he was told in writing is enough.

Duras did not understand the reason *The Lover* had such an impact on the literary world. She writes,

I can't understand why The Lover has had such success, has reached a wider public than my previous books. I've been launched like some sort of 'star.' And I tell you something: this exhibition of my person, this turning me into something almost sacred, feels closer to death than anything I've experienced up to this date.

Verena Andermatt Conley in her essay *Duras and the Scene of Writing* examines the possibility of why this work was so well received. She claims,

In what seems to be Duras' progressive stripping away of detail, descriptions, in order to accede to a primitive scene, the scene of a coming onto writing, of the shaping of the artist, L'Amant is a curious mixture of writing a l'eau de rose from Elle magazine or an afternoon soap opera and another writing, decisive, definitive, which— to paraphrase the writer—does not talk about things but goes into them.

As was the case with all of Duras' later writings, she turned her emotions on a subject into a poetic statement. This depiction of deep sentiment is exactly what sets *The Lover* apart from all of her earlier works and makes it so compelling to the reader.

From Duras' appraisal of her work, we come to understand that she was not lost in the ego based motivations of many autobiographically based authors. Instead, it can be understood that Duras simply created literature from the most enlightened temperament that she could muster and spilled out her emotions onto the written page.

The North China Lover or *Amant de la Chine du Nord,* was completed in May of 1991. Many critics and literary historians believe that Duras wrote this book because she was fired from the job of screenwriter for the film, based on her novel, *The Lover.* This dismissal came due to artistic differences between the film's director, Jean-Jacques Annaud and Duras. In any case, the book opens with Duras reflecting about the fact that her first lover, the Chinese man, had died.

> *I learned that he had been dead for some years. That was May 1990, a year ago now. I had never thought of him as dead.*

She goes on to state,

> *I stopped the work I was doing. I wrote the story of the North China lover and the child: it wasn't quite there in The Lover, I hadn't given them enough time. Writing this book made me deliriously happy. The novel kept me a year, enclosed me in that year of the love between the Chinese man and the child.*

The North China Lover is quite different from *The Lover* in terms of style and application. It is not a random stream of consciousness narrative, but, instead, is relatively linear in its structure and storyline. The book does not reminisce about various life timeframes of "I," changing tense and story structure in mid-sentence. It does, however, take on the advanced quality of style *The Lover* possessed in the fact that the author will at one point be describing the story in the here and now and then move into a state of remembrance in order to allow the reader to understand the book is being composed from memory. For example,

> *She remembers. She is the last to remember. She still hears the sound of the sea in the room. And she remembers having written that. As she remembers the Chinese street. She even remembers writing that the sea was present that day in the lovers' room. She wrote the words: the sea, and three other words—the words simply and beyond compare.*

Though the story does take the reader into additional areas of Duras' life and/or imagination, one is not left with the sense of truly knowing her and being deeply involved in her life and experiences, as was the case with *The Lover.* The style of not taking the reader deeply into the characters is not something new in Duras' literature. Trista Selous in her essay, *The Withering Away of Character,* states,

> *Even in her early works, Duras does not go into great detail in the creation of 'character'. The reader is not given detailed descriptions of the figures in the novel: their history, idiosyncrasies of speech, the color of their eyes, etc.*

Stylistically, the most interesting artistic quality about *The North China Lover* is the fact that Duras, refers to her character as "She," or "The

Child," as we have seen in the previously cited paragraph. Her lover, in this novel is simply referred to as, "The Chinese," her mother as, "The Mother," her brothers as, "The Little or Younger Brother," and "The Older Brother."

In the passage,

> *The little brother comes back from dancing. He asks his sister to dance. They have always danced together, it's marvelous to see: the little brother dances as though in his sleep, apparently without even realizing he is dancing. He doesn't look at his sister and his sister doesn't look at him, either. They dance together without knowing how to dance. They will never in their lives dance like this again.*

One can see how she uses this terminology to artistically describe herself and her brother. These abstract descriptions keep the reader away from the soul of Duras' character in the novel and this is obviously intentional.

The exception to the previously described non-emotion based writing style is witnessed in Duras' introduction to the book, when she writes in the first-person. She writes,

> *I could never have imagined the Chinese dying, his body dying, his sex, his hands. For a whole year I went back to the days when I would cross the Mekong River, on the ferry to Vinh-Long.*

In this passage the reader witnesses how the memory of her first love and the geographic location of her love affair still haunted Duras.

When studying the fact that Duras refers to her literary characters in this novel as, "The Something," it can be understood that she was essentially separating them from herself, making that particular individual distant. The characters in this novel are, therefore, no longer people but simply objects.

It is apparent that though Duras possessed a life-long affection and remembrance of her first lover, he eventually, through time, became reduced to simply being referred to as an object defined by his ethnic origin. As if almost racist, Duras herself degrades him to this racially defined level.

This racial difference between Duras and her lover was obviously a defining point in their relationship. This fact is clearly depicted as having arisen more on the part of "The Chinese" than from her own adolescent ideology. None-the-less, it is always a factor depicted in her novels relating to this man.

From this literary description, the reader can come to understand that throughout the world racial definition is a very prominent defining life factor on both the part of the Caucasians and especially the Asians, even when placed in the realm of artistic writings. This relationship, in all of Duras' books about the subject was based on this comparison, this duality.

In *The North China Lover,* Duras embellishes this separatism and duality between her and her first love. She does so in such a flagrant manner that it is as if she was blatantly removing control away from him and taking control over this racially based subject for the first time in her life.

As depicted in all of her books dealing with her love affair with this man, it was she who was continually on the lower end of the racial spectrum, and she who was rejected for being Caucasian. In fact, it was Duras who this man eventually left for another woman of the same Chinese heritage as himself.

Duras in this book, whether knowingly or not, shifts the tables on this man and their love affair. Though the storyline does not radically change from when it was first told in *The Sea Wall* or *The Lover,* Duras, none-the-less, by the use of racial and other singularly defining titles reduces any thoughts or actions this man may have expressed or taken to being that of acts of a non-being, simply deeds of an entity.

If this novel were not so obviously autobiographical, one could surmise that these defining titles given to characters is an attempt to depict the more metaphysical realm of Yin and Yang understanding; the duality of life: the strong versus the weak, the white as opposed to the black, the positive and the negative, the male and the female. But, as this novel is autobiographical in the telling of its tale, this level of possible mystical perception is removed, and it becomes simply a story being told from the singular perspective of one individual.

This defining of individuals, including herself, as "The" can be viewed in the deeper psychological levels, however, as one seeking to remove oneself from the realities and activity which has taken one through the course of one's life. As is the case with all dysfunctional families, the child often times wishes to escape the grasp of the dominant family members. This too was Duras' case. In this novel, as if almost to complete the final separation, she describes herself as: "Her," or "The Child." From this literary action, not only she, but also her family and her first lover become something distant and not real.

When eroticism is viewed in *The North China Lover,* one sees that it is not essentially different from that of her other, earlier, novels; descriptive, yet, sparely worded to the degree that no word is unnecessarily used.

> *He is sitting in front of her; she is standing. She lowers her eyes. He takes her dress by the hem, lifts it off of her. Then he slips off her child's white cotton underpants. He throws the dress and underpants on the chair. He takes his hands off her body, looks at it. Looks at her. She, no. She keeps her eyes lowered, she lets him look.*
> *He gets up. She stays standing before him. She waits. He sits down again. He strokes, but just barely, her skinny body. Her child's breasts, her stomach. He closes his eyes like a blind man. He stops. He takes away his hands. He opens his eyes. Very low he says: "You aren't sixteen years. It isn't true."*

Bearing in mind what was previously stated about the psychologically based removal of "I" Duras illustrates in *The North China Lover,* it can none-the-less be witnessed that she allows the reader to experience a deeper side of "The Child," when it comes to the subject matter of eroticism. In this area she writes in a fashion to show that she,

"The Child," does possess deep feelings and is motivated by more than simply the obvious level of adolescent sexuality.

Duras writes,

> *She does it. As she comes, she says his name in Chinese. She has done it. They look at each other, look at each other until the tears come. And for the first time in her life she says the standard words for saying it— the words in the books, the movies, life, for every lover. "I love you."*

Love, and/or the running away from love, and ultimately the denial of love, is what this novel is based upon. This novel defines Duras' understanding of love, which comes from the mind of a mature individual gained at the expense of an adolescent girl.

Liliane Papin in her essay *Place of Writing, Place of Love writes,*

> *When Marguerite Duras' characters are in love, nothing can stop them, nothing can restrain them, not even those they love. Love for them is not and cannot be a way of possessing, it cannot be turned back toward the self. On the contrary, it entails the discovery of the basic difference, the basic alacrity of the other, the respect for his or her freedom: her characters never fail to respect that fundamental freedom.*

This erroneous statement made by Papin is in contrast to the style of literary love Duras generally embraces. Duras' love is not based in freedom. It is based in one individual possessing the power over the other and the continual battle for supremacy until one character or the other emerges victorious.

Love to Duras, in her literary works, is measured by the power of erotic sensuality and not simply by the emotion known as love. The emotion of love is only referenced in context to sexuality, whether it is in progress, impending, or desired. From this conquest her characters are dominated. When one cannot gain desired control over the other, that character leaves the other one as a final blow in the battle.

At the completion of *The North China Lover* Duras details suggestions for how she would like to see this novel turned into a film. This was not the first time she had added this postscript of filming ideas to one of her books. It was added to several of her earlier novels. The inclusion of these ideas, however, leaves one speculating upon Duras' true motivation for the writing of this novel. As previously stated, it is believed that Duras wrote *The North China Lover* in direct response to her being fired as the screenwriter from the film version of *The Lover*. With the restructuring of the storyline in *The North China Lover* and her written concepts for the making of this novel into a film, she allowed the film version of *The Lover* to appear somewhat inaccurate.

Perhaps what is most interesting about Duras finishing the novel with filming ideas is the fact that she writes the sentence in the introduction,

I became a novelist all over again.

Was she actually a novelist again, after having become a playwright, screenwriter, and director? It does not appear as if she was. Instead, though she continued to have the ability to write enthralling novels, her mind was really on that of the visual images which feature films solely possess.

Within the pages of Duras' novel, *The Ravishing of Lol Stein,* which was first published in France as *Le Ravissement de Lol V. Stein* in 1964, one has the ability to witness what may be viewed as an ideal literary work depicting the transitional period of Duras' literary career from that of a traditional novelist to a truly artistic literary figure. The novels opening paragraphs set the stage for this artistic work by immediately detailing the facts of this story. Duras writes,

> *Lol Stein was born here in South Tahla, and she spent a good part of her youth in this town. Her father was a professor at the university. Lol has a brother nine years older than she—I have never seen him—they say he lives in Paris. Her parents are dead. I have never heard anything especially noteworthy about Lol Stein's childhood, even from Tatiana Karl, her best friend during their school years together.*

On initial observation this passage may appear to be traditional in novel storyline and structure. The interesting fact to observe, however, lies in the method of how Duras, by this point in her literary career, had developed the ability, within a single paragraph, to first detail the profession of a parent, then to describe how this individual was, in fact, of high position (a professor), and then by the end of the same paragraph explain that the person is, in fact, no longer living.

Alfred Cismaru, in his text, *Marguerite Duras,* claims that the style of writing presented in, *The Ravishing of Lol Stein,* is the only admirable quality about this novel. He writes,

> *Actually, Marguerite Duras' ability to maneuver words into catching touching combinations ranging   from sentence to paragraph length is the only pleasing quality of this novel.*

In this novel, Duras is no longer bound by the common constraints of literary "Time-Frame" and traditional story explanation, and moves literature to a new level by her subtle ability to "Time-Shift" without making the story unduly complicated. This subtle form of literary depiction continues hence in all of Duras' later novels, as she continues to develop further methods of artistic storytelling, which embraces shifting time frame, and first and third person story telling.

Within the first few pages of this novel, Duras virtually tells the whole story of how Lol, at the age of nineteen, meets a man, of twenty-five, Michael Richardson, of wealthy parents and falls in love with him only to be jilted when he chooses to be with her friend Tatiana. The most interesting element of this type of writing is that the reader is allowed to know what story is to be told before ever reading deeply into the novel, almost as if "A Preview" of what is to come is laid out.

From this "Preview," the knowledgeable Duras reader will immediately see the parallel between the story of *Lol Stein* and Duras' own autobiographical works of her love affair with an older, wealthy Chinese man. From this comparison, one can immediately understand how this love affair, which took place in Duras' adolescence, motivated much of her later literature, even if the subject matter was set in a different geographical location and other characters were used to tell the story; the influence was, none-the-less, obvious.

Marilyn R. Schuster, in her essay, *Criminals of Love: From Interrogations of Desire to a Narrative of Silence,* states,

> *In the early novels, Duras used a third-person narrative situated in a female character's consciousness that erupted into the first person in moments of particular urgency, inscribing a split feminine subject moving from observed to observer. In the Ravishing of Lol Stein, told in the masculine first-person narrative, the third person erupts at moments of fantasy and desire, signaling a split masculine subject, moving from observer to observed.*

Duras, in this novel, is quick to reference two points she continually returns to throughout much of her literature, that of obvious sexuality and that of an individual verging on madness.

> *Tatiana does not believe that this fabled Town Beach Ball was so overwhelmingly responsible for Lol Stein's illness. No, Tatiana Karl traces the origins of that illness back further, further than the beginning of their friendship. They were*

47

latent in Lol Stein, but kept from emerging by the deep affection with which she had always been surrounded both at home and, later, at school. She says that in school— and she wasn't the only person to think so— there was already something lacking in Lol, something which kept her from being in Tatiana's words, "there."

When viewing this novel as a whole and complete work, the reader is allowed to see that what is set into place in the "Preview" sets the stage for what is to be told throughout the novel. The area worthy of notice is the fact that the same themes, particularly that of mental imbalance, reappear throughout the work and are described in virtually the same words that appear in the opening paragraphs. This literary technique is used so effectively that it seems to eliminate the need for secondary description.

Personally, Tatiana did not believe that Lol Stein's insanity could be traced back solely to that ball, she traced its origins back further in Lol's life back to her youth, she saw it as stemming from somewhere else. In school, she says, there was something lacking in Lol, she was already then strangely incomplete, she had lived her early years as though she were waiting for something she might, but never did, become.

It is difficult to discern whether or not Duras did this as a conscious reaffirming literary technique or whether it simply happened as a

"Stream of Consciousness" writing technique. None-the-less, this technique of reaffirmation adds continued definition to the storyline and serves as a reminder to the reader of the motivating factors that control the central character.

Duras is not unique in her literary obsession with impending insanity. This is an area of thought which has been transversed by many an author. What perhaps is most interesting is the way in which Duras approaches this subject. She writes of it in an literary abstractness, with little regard for what may have caused this mindset or what the individual may actually be experiencing. Instead, she always speaks of it, as "Something else" not real—an object as opposed to an experience.

This type of descriptive process is in sharp contrast to the vivid style Duras uses in describing family involvements and pending or active sexual relationships. The reader can only assume that this area of thought, and the subject of insanity itself, is too close to home for Duras to delve deeply into it.

Duras, in all of her autobiographically based novels, deals with this pending insanity. It is obviously an area of thought that has haunted her since her childhood and on into her adult life, as well.

Duras' approach to eroticism, in this novel, is not as blatant and exact as in some of her later works. The foundation of her subtly erotic, yet highly descriptive method of depicting sexual acts was, however, well formed by this period in her literary career.

He hides Tatiana Karl's face beneath the sheets, and thus has her headless body at his disposal, at his entire disposal. He turns the

49

body this way and that, raises it, does with it whatever he desires, spreads the limbs or draws them in close, stares fixedly at its irreversible beauty, enters it, remains motionless, awaits being trapped into forgetfulness, forgetfulness is there.

As one can see, she was able to describe the act of sexual involvement so artistically as to raise it above the physical act itself, and creating an artistic visual image in the mind of the reader.

Many critics did not view this novel as a transitional work. Instead, they did not find it a rewarding piece of literature as can be witnessed in Alfred Cismaru's review. He writes,

There is very little please or review in Madame Duras' 1964 fiction publication. Although there is no connection between Le Ravissement de Lol V. Stein and Les Impudents, not since her debut literature did she write a less effective novel.

In spite of the author's established reputation by this time and in spite of the usual critical acclaim bestowed upon her work, Marguerite Duras saw her cryptic story of a mentally deranged women greeted with sparing comment if not outright indifference.

Duras commonly found great reverence for her work both in France and abroad. This was generally based in her artistically pushing the boundaries of the commonly perceived understanding of literature to new and uncharted ground. France, having a much deeper tradition of

50

erotic art and literature than much of the rest of the world, found her detailed depictions of sexuality enticing. None-the-less, Duras too found critics, including French literary critics, who possessed negative perceptions of her work based primarily on her lack of conventional story formula. In a case such as this novel, they did not choose to view the idealistic simplicity of the storyline and instead chose to focus upon what they perceived as its lack of depth.

Destroy She Said was originally published in France as *Detruire Dit-Elle* in 1969. This novel, as is the case with several other of Duras' works, was eventually produced as a film in France. Though it was produced as a film, Duras obviously did not predict this occurrence, as the culmination of the novel is, "Note for Performance," where the setting for this book being turned into a play is described.

There are four main characters in this book. Duras in her writing of this novel obviously kept characters to a minimum so casting this book into a play would be more easily accomplished. She states,

> *No need for any people but the main characters. The others can be suggested by the falling of light on various objects: chaises-lounges in a circle, or separate, or facing each other, empty. In the dining room, white cloths on the tables supposed to be occupied.*

In this novel, dialogue is the driving factor that sets the stage as the participants interact. Through this dialogue, one realizes the peculiarity of each of the individual characters. The peculiarity is based on the fact that the characters are in a hotel, which seemingly symbolizes a mental institution. Again, as in *The Ravishing of Lol Stein,* Duras refers to madness in an abstract fashion.

Destroy She Said, opens, clearly defining the abnormal minds of the individual characters.

> *An overcast sky. The bay windows shut. From where he is in the dinning room he can't see outside. But she can. She is looking out. Her table touches the windowsill. The light makes her screw up her eyes. They move to and fro. Some of the other guests are watching the tennis matches too. But he can't see. He hasn't asked to be moved to another table though. She doesn't know she is being watched. It rained this morning about five. Today the air the balls thud through is close and heavy. She is wearing a summer dress. The book is in front of her. Begun since he arrived? or before? Beside the book are two bottles of white pills. She takes some every meal.*

Duras writes this book, no doubt, as an attempt to stir the senses of the reader, initially by the character descriptions and then through the character's conversations. The structure of the dialogue presented in this novel is beyond what could be considered normal discourse. This lack of normality and the abstract responses that are given to questions posed is Duras revealing that normality is not relevant in term of artistic literature. In fact, one needs to step beyond normality and common understanding to come to any true conception of the art of life.

Instead of simply writing about the characters from a sane state of mind, Duras enters into their minds, and talks as they would. In this novel, conversation takes the path of the short interchanges; such as,

> *"I'm so happy you're here," he says. She looks around. Then brings her eyes back, slowly. "Destroy," she says. He smiles at her.*

Trista Selous, in her book on Duras, *The Other Woman,* writes,

> *The obscurity of Detruire, dit-elle lies in what might be described as the minimalism of the construction of the figures, Alissa, Stein, Max Thor, Elizabeth Alione, and the hotel in which they are staying. The description of these figures and their hotel is in Duras' familiar style of very short sentences describing primarily what is visible.*

As Selous states, this novel is written with Duras minimalism. With this, the physical setting and the characters are allowed to simply exist without going into deep discussion for the reasoning behind their existence.

In the following conversational segment, the novel's characters are planning to take a walk in the mysterious forest that surrounds the hotel. This mysterious forest is reminiscent of that which is metaphorically described in so many novels, as the realm of vague uncertainty, where anything may and probably will happen. This forest is especially descriptive in the sense that these characters are not of normal mind. Thus, their stepping out into it the forest obviously means their return to insanity. The characters, in this case, however, ultimately decide to walk on the seemingly safe grounds of the hotel, instead. This obviously is an area of known mental and emotional safety.

> *"Let's stay in the grounds," Elizabeth Alione says.*
> *Silence.*
> *"As you like," Alissa says.*
> *Silence. They retrace their steps.*
> *"To go back to what we were saying,"*
> *Stein says. "Total destruction."*

This style of on going discourse not only defines the characters in this book, but drives the story, as well.

This novel extensively uses the, "He said—She said," structure. It is at times a bit distracting to the actual storyline; not dissimilar from Hemingway's *For Whom the Bell Tolls,* where the amount of dialogue almost overpowers the actual storyline. In fact, Hemingway may well have been an influence on Duras in this particular period of her literary career. Though the dialogue does not necessarily mirror that of Hemingway, it, none-the-less, is reminiscent of some of the subtle erotic styling he also displayed in the aforementioned novel.

Eroticism in this novel is referenced in terms of dialogue. Though the erotic is not the driving factor of this novel, as is the case with other of her works, Duras, never the less, due to her apparent love for the various forms of the erotic, details, in the form of dialogue, an area of eroticism not commonly discussed in her other works, that of voyeurism.

> *"We make love," Alissa says. "Every night we make love."*
> *"I know," says Stein. "You leave the window open and I see you."*
> *"He leaves it open for you. To see us."*

The Malady of Death was first published in Paris in 1982. It was then translated and published into English in 1986. This book takes an abstract path in the telling of its tale—abstract, almost to the degree of a Zen Koan. This story is non-linear in nature, as its tale unfolds simultaneously throughout the pages.

The Malady of Death opens in mature Duras fashion, with prose type verse setting the stage for what is to be depicted. The first passage of this works states,

> *You wouldn't have known her, you'd have seen her everywhere at once, in a hotel, in a street, in a train, in a bar, in a book, in a film, in yourself, your inmost self, when your sex grew erect in the night, seeking somewhere to put itself, somewhere to shed its tears.*

In this opening sentence, the reader is artistically told of the overall essence of the work: a enigmatic woman, intermingled with the implications of male sexual ideology, "When your sex grew erect in the night, somewhere to put itself, somewhere to shed its tears." The most interesting observation which may be made from this opening passage is how Duras had the ability to depict abstract literature not only from the perspective of a woman, but from the viewpoint and mindset of a man, as well. Few modern women authors choose to enter into the psyche of a man. Instead, they focus their literature solely on the perspective of the female. Duras, however, due to a life of experience was able to casually illustrate a literary situation, touching the source of male sexuality, and, to do so in a casual passing sense, instead of being overtly gregarious or exceedingly contrived with her chosen words.

The erotic details of this story are often told in a metaphoric fashion, rather than use of exact descriptive wording. This is what makes this work truly artistic in its execution. This style of storytelling allows the reader to be deeply drawn into the mystery that is associated with the act of sexual intercourse, without being overwhelmed by the book's intent. Duras writes,

> *She says: Look. She parts her legs, and in the hollow between you see the dark night at last. Once the stage has been set for sexual union to occur, Duras gives the reader an artistic, emotional description of the act. Then you stroke more quickly. And you see that her thighs are opening to give your hand more room, so that you can stroke better than before. And suddenly, in a moan, you see pleasure come upon her, take possession of her, make her arch up from the bed. You look intently at what you have just done to her body. Then you see it fall back inert on the white of the bed.*

In the cases such as the above passages, what Duras details could never be considered pornographic. Instead, her writing remains ambiguous. This space for interpretation is what makes this book truly interesting, and one of Duras' mature efforts in artistic eroticism.

Not only does Duras artistically describe the erotic but she additionally goes into the formation and basis of emotion, particularly that of love. Duras writes,

> *She answers: Perhaps a sudden lapse in the logic of the universe. She says: Through a mistake, for instance. She says: Never through an act of will. You ask: Could the emotion of loving come from other things too? You beg her to say. She says: It can come from anything, from the flight of a night bird, from a sleep, from a dream of sleep, from the approach of death, from a word, from a crime, of itself, from oneself, often without knowing how.*

With this, we understand that Duras contemplates the basis for the emotion of love. As all advanced novelists do, Duras also intermingles her own perplexing universal questions into the storyline. This allows the reader to delve deeply into not only the mind of the characters but into Duras' questioning mind, as well.

The book culminates with,

> *If I ever filmed this text I'd want the weeping by the sea to be shot in such a way that the white turmoil of the waves is seen almost*

simultaneously with the man's face. There should be a correlation between the white of the sheets and the white of the sea. The sheets should be a prior image of the sea. All this by way of general suggestion.

To view Duras at this stage in her writing career, after having written and directed several plays and screenplays, in addition to having seen her international award winning film, Hiroshima, Me Amour produced, we see that her mind went to the visual precepts of a storyline and not just to that of the written page. As is often the case with a screenwriter, who envisions his work in his mind's eye and then puts it to paper with the intention of the film's production company being able to find ways in which to orchestrate that vision, this was obviously the case with Duras at this point in her literary career. She wrote her novels with the intention of them being turned into feature films.

Blues Eyes, Black Hair, Les Yuex Blues Cheveux Noirs, published in 1987, is a novel with obsessive passion and mature Duras eroticism at its center. This tale follows the obsessions of a man whom instantly falls in love with another man, upon first glance. As his desire for this man cannot be lived, he substitutes a woman for this man and he unleashes his misplaced perverse passion upon her. Definite in its point of view and story content, this novel is one of Duras' most explicit in terms of neurotic/erotic subject matter.

The novel begins with the passage,

A SUMMER EVENING, says the actor, seems to be at the heart of the affair.

The implication of this opening statement is two fold. First of all, again we see Duras setting the stage for the theatrical presentation of this novel. This fact is exemplified within this novel as, at various points, Duras shifts to giving stage commands mid-text. The second indirect suggestion of this opening statement is that it sets the mind of the reader into a state of disassociation from firm reality. Thus, the novel is allowed to be read from a dispassionate frame of reference—a factor that is rarely the case with Duras literature.

This novel is dedicated to Yann Andrea Steiner, Duras' gay younger lover, who she met after recovering from an alcohol-induced coma. Thus, the comparison between what takes place with the third-person central female character, in the pages of this novel, and that of the life of Duras, herself, cannot be overlooked. As Duras admittedly turns to her life for literary inspiration, how she depicts this female character allows a deeply perceived view into the mind and lifestyle of an aging Duras.

Marilyn R. Schuster, details some of the underlying aspects of this text in her essay, *Return to Writing: Duras Becomes Duras,*

This coincides with the arrival of Yann Andrea in her life and has inevitably led readers to consider them, especially Blue Eyes, Black Hair which is dedicated to Andrea and was published after the success of The Lover, as an insight into their life together. The theme of male homosexuality is a screen, however, like the other erotic texts, these texts interrogate a particular construction of heterosexuality as imagined through a feminine subjectivity. Duras uses the figure of the male homosexual to confirm that sexual union is a cruel deception, that sexuality reiterates an essential isolation of the individual, a disconnection between lovers. Absence, violence, and solitude have always marked what Duras has called the tragedy of passion.

In the Duras novel, *Yann Andrea Steiner*, named after her final lover, Duras in a complication of extremely short stories details aspects of her relationship with this man. From the comparison between this depicted illustration of her relationship and the novel, *Blue Eyes, Black Hair*, one can, in fact, view the similarities between the seemingly fictional relationship and the aspects of obsessive neurotic love which haunted Duras throughout her life. Duras writes,

Sometimes I was afraid as soon as you woke up. Like all men every day, even if only for a few seconds, you become a woman-killer. It might happen any day. Sometimes you were as frightening as a lost hunter or an escaped criminal. And this made the people around me afraid for me sometimes. And for me it was always there I was afraid of you. Every day, for a few brief moments you were not even aware of, I was afraid when you looked at me.

As can be observed from the previous paragraph, Duras embraced fear in most of her personal relationships. The neurotic obsessional motivation for her to be in a relationship based in fear, can only be seen as being based in her own lack of emotional stability and self actualization. It does clearly reveal, however, a motivational characteristic for not only her own psyche but for her novelistic female characters, as well.

Duras, again, refers to Steiner in another short story, *L'Homme atlantique*. She writes,

> *It is the summer of 1986. I'm writing the story. Throughout the summer, every day, sometimes in the evening, sometimes at night. It is then that Yann enters a period of crying out loud, of shouting. He types out the book, two hours each day. In the book, I'm eighteen, I'm in love with a man who loathes my desire, my body. Yann types as I dictate. While he types, he doesn't shout. That happens afterwards.*

Again, in Duras' own words, she spells out the intensity of a relationship that is based in distaste and anger. From this depiction, we see that her lover is, in fact, the one who types her later literary works. Thus, to a non-specified degree he is in her employee.

To put this all in to context, we can follow this short story a bit further. Duras continues,

> *I hardly ever see him, this man, Yann. He's hardly ever there, in our apartment by the sea. He goes for walks. During the day he covers different distances, each several*

times. He goes from hill to hill. He visits the large hotels, he seeks out beautiful men. He meets several handsome bartenders.

What is obvious in the life of Duras is that she has met a younger homosexual man, who sees Duras as a mother figure. Duras at this time is sixty-eight years old. She obviously supports him financially and does not hinder him from meeting and associating with other men, his chosen desire. Yet, Duras is the financial mainstay of the relationship and expects certain physical gratifications because of this. Steiner obviously feels negative emotional pressure based in Duras' power over him, as he obviously possesses unresolved psychological issues with his mother. Though Steiner types Duras' books for her, he hates it, as it is not simply a job to him but an inflicted physical relationship where he is forced to confront demons that he is not prepared to deal with; if he were, he would not have found himself in this predicament. His yelling, his crying, and his intimidation of her express Steiner's anger towards Duras. Duras, never-the-less, is locked into the relationship; the emotional reasoning is most probably the reliving of her youth—a younger man and a lonely, solitary older woman...

In the book, *Practicalities,* Duras details her ideology about men and their sexual orientation. She says,

> *I think men's behavior to women is generallybrutal and high-handed. But that doesn't necessarily mean men are brutal and high-handed—only that men are like that in the context of the heterosexual couple.*

Because they are uneasy in that relationship.

Here we see that Duras, having lived a long life and obviously having experienced many varying types of relationships, gives justification for her interaction with Steiner. As almost as if to persuade her reader that what she claims is fact, she details her ideology about heterosexual relationships, thus, giving birth to a perceived validity for her alternative type of lover.

Duras idealizes this relationship in her writings at times. She writes,

We went to bed with the moon in a dark blue sky. It was the next day that we made love. You came to my bedroom. We didn't say a word. We were fueled by the childish body of Theodora Kats, that crippled body, its bright eyes, its cries to its mother before it was shot in the neck by the German soldier in charge of the camp. Afterwards you said my body was incredibly young. I've hesitated about writing that down for publication. But I hadn't the strength not to. I write down things I don't understand, too. I leave them in my books and reread them later and then they take on a meaning. I said people always told me that, even the North China Lover said the same thing, and I was only fourteen at the time.

In the previous passage, written by Duras, she obviously desired to believe what had been said to her and then record it for posterity. The statement

63

obviously represented to her that she was still found attractive in her aging years. As has been the case with so many men throughout history, due to their position of wealth or notoriety they possessed the power to obtain a younger mate. This was obviously the case of Duras. The previous statement was obviously one used to compliment her. Whether or not it was believed by the speaker can only be speculated upon. None-the-less, its effect upon Duras accomplished what Yann had intended it to do, flatter his primary means of support.

In the pages of *Blue Eyes, Black Hair,* Duras references the dysfunctional relationship between the two central characters: the female and the gay male. Though no exact comparisons are drawn between Duras, Steiner, and this couple, as Steiner was the typist, the underlying current of a psychologically perverse relationship is spelled out in these pages filled with eroticism.

Duras writes,

> *Every evening she brings her body to the room, undresses it, places it in the middle of the yellow light. She covers her face with the black silk. It's when she's supposed to be asleep that he looks at her what other men have done to her body: often there are marks, but very slight and unintentional. This particular day the scent of the man is very strong, though mixed with the smell of sweet cigarettes, make-up. He lifts the black scarf. Her face is drawn.*

The scarf that the woman uses to hide her face can be understood to be the veil in which Duras hid herself from realizing the true desire of her gay lover and to hide the fact of her age from Steiner. The scarf is eventually removed by the lover. This can be seen as symbolizing Duras revealing herself to the man and his coming to terms with his misplaced affection for the woman. These literary symbols obviously represented hopeful speculation on the part of Duras.

Duras in the later part of her, specifically, literary career, tended to write short, single or two page statements, and short stories, as opposed to detailed novels, as was the case with her earlier work. Duras, continued to evolve her style until it became more and more abstract and less dependent on accepted patterns of story content and literary structure. After *The Lover,* however, Duras never again was able to achieve the high standard of flowing Zen like literature that its text conveyed. Instead, she continued along a literary path of impacting her readers with intense emotional content and unique story framework until her death in 1996.

In the work entitled, *Hanoi,* Duras details the possible birth of her mindset towards male/female relationships and her psychological basis for eroticism.

> *And there was Hanoi too, which I've never talked about, I don't know why. Before Vinh Long, six years before, there was Hanoi. In the house my mother had bought on the Little Lake. At that time my mother took paying guests. Vietnamese and Laotian boys aged about twelve or thirteen. One afternoon one of them asked me to go with him to a "hidey-hole." I wasn't afraid, so I*

went. The place was on the edge of the lake, between a couple of wooden huts that must have belonged to the house. I can remember a kind of narrow passage between the walls made of planks. This was where the defloration in the book took place: among the bathing huts. They became the sea, but the pleasure was there even then, its nature already essentially foreshadowed. And also unforgettable even then, in the body of a child light-years away from understanding what it was, but already receiving the signal, even then. The next day my mother sent the Vietnamese boy packing—I'd thought it my duty to tell her everything, confess everything. I can remember it all quite plainly. It is as if I was dishonored by having been touched. I was four years old. He was eleven and a half—not yet pubescent. His prick was still limp and soft. He told me what to do. I took hold of it, he put his hand on mine, and our two hands stroked it more and more strongly. Then he stopped. I've never forgotten the feel of its shape in my hand, or its warmth. Or the child's face, eyes shut, martyr-like, waiting for, straining towards, a pleasure still out of reach.

Whereas many females would find this action and the memory of it negatively haunting, Duras saw in it as the basis and first definition of her sexual desire. Thus, from her childhood forward Duras lived the life of desire to its fullest limit.

Marguerite Duras died on 3 March 1996 in Paris. She was eighty-one years old.

As one searches for the essence of Duras' eroticism, one comes to realize, when viewing all of her writing as a whole, that it, "The Erotic," is not so much based in elements of love or even lust, it is instead rooted in the abstract realms of the psychological. The psychological basis for her delving into the erotic can be charted back to her childhood in Southeast Asia, when, if one chooses to accept and believe the stories she tells as fact, was an environment where a young girl found herself at odds with not only the cultural environment but with her family, as well. As this type of atmosphere would cause even the most astute of intellects to emerge with a certain amount of dysfunctionality, it too, no doubt affected Duras.

Marguerite Duras, obviously had much affection for her mother, though at times it was a trying relationship. Duras' father, virtually non-existent in her life, played a very minor role in her growing up, though obviously his existence set the stage for the location where her childhood and adolescence took place. Then there were her two brothers: one she loved, the other she did not. From all of these highly detailed and described factors, the Duras reader can see how she, seeking acceptance and purpose, entered into a teenage love affair with an older man, in order, not only to gain the father figure which was lacking from her life, but also to set about on a course of teenage rebellion—a common occurrence no matter where the geographical location or degree of social status.

Propelled by all of these elements, Duras obviously set about on a life course to artistically depict a relatively short-lived event in her life, that of her love affair with a rich and mysterious man. She obviously took the memory of this experience into all of her later relationships, comparing them all to this turbulent love affair. As is often the case in life, if relationships are allowed to go on for a long period of time and then die out slowly, the participants do not hold such a high reverence for what took place. When, on the other hand, a relationship is very passionate and then ends quickly, for any number of reasons, at least one of the participants is left feeling a longing sense of passion and loving remembrance for what took place. This was obviously the case of Marguerite Duras. On this point, she focused her literary career.

Charles Bukowski

Henry Charles Bukowski, Jr., was born in Andernach, Germany on 16 August 1920 to Henry Bukowski, an American GI, and Katherine Fett, a native German, whose brother managed a canteen serving the American troops. Upon Henry Sr.'s discharge from the service, he returned with his new family to California where his father, Leonard Bukowski, had emigrated from Germany in the 1880's. Henry Sr. began the job of a milk deliveryman.

Due to Henry Sr.'s obsessive behavior and his mother's German accent, the young Bukowski had a trying childhood, though he lived in a middle class environment in the central section of Los Angeles. Hank, as he was called by his classmates, was continually taunted. Neeli Cherkovski in his biography, *Hank: The Life of Charles Bukowski* Biography, writes.

> *He was constantly rebuffed by the boys. "Hey Heinie! What are you doing, Heinie?" One of them said, "We don't want to play with you. Go back to Germany with all those krauts."*

The young Bukowski developed throughout his childhood with a nagging sense of alienation. This understanding was added to by Henry Sr.'s continual shooing off of other children from his lawn. When other children were allowed in his house, their actions were dominated by his father's watchful eye. Cherkovski explains,

Hank's birthday parties were ruined by his father. Children were welcomed into his house, given paper hats to wear and directed toward different party games like pin the tail on the donkey. But it quickly became Henry's show. He hovered over the young guests like a Prussian officer. There would be ice cream and cake, little paper napkins printed with Happy Birthday. Henry made sure the kids didn't spill any cake on the floor or drip ice cream on the rug. If they did, he shouted in a way guaranteed to frighten them. Katherine would stand off to one side, passively letting her husband do as he wished. Even during the games, he commanded: "You must play politely." If they became noisy, he shouted them down, ordering them back into their chairs.

Henry Sr. was a strict disciplinarian, not only with the young Bukowski but with his wife, as well. This combined with the fact that he constantly complained about his job, his co-worker, and his transfer to different milk delivery routes, haunted the life of the young Bukowski. Not only did he find an increasingly developed sense of separation and isolation from his peers, he equally began to dislike his family's attitude.

During his teen years, Bukowski developed an intense case of acne; there appeared to be no cure for as it continued to worsen. This again provided his fellow classmates with ammunition for ridicule but additionally caused him to be alienated from those of the opposite sex. This combination of early experiences and developed inter-relationships with his family and the external world can clearly be seen to have greatly influenced the later development of Bukowski as an author and a human being. Cherkovski. details,

> *In 1937, during the last semester of the school year, Hank began drinking. Because he looked older than his age, he occasionally went into the bars in downtown L.A., and found whiskey to his liking,*

This early endeavor into alcoholism, at the age of seventeen, would dominate the rest of Bukowski's life. Bukowski personally details his early experiences with alcohol in his novel, *Notes of a Dirty Old Man*. He states,

> *I began drinking about 17 with the older boys who roamed the streets and robbed gas stations and liquor stores. they thought my disgust with everything was a lack of fear, that my non-complaining was a soulful bravado. I was popular and I didn't care whether I was popular or not. I was Frozen. they set great quantities of whiskey and beer and wine in front of me. I drank them down. nothing could get me drunk, really and finally drunk, the others would be falling to the floor, fighting, singing, swaggering, and I would sit quietly at the table draining another glass, feeling less and less with them, feeling lost, but not painfully so. just electric light and sound and bodies and little more.*

It was at this same period of time when Charles Bukowski was experiencing his first steps towards profound alcoholism that he composed his first short story. Certainly, it could not have been predicted that the fateful events of Bukowski's seventeenth year would dictate and define the rest of his life.

Bukowski spent the early years of his adult life roaming the country, taking temporal employment, getting drunk, and to a lesser degree writing poetry and short stories. In 1944, he was first published in the magazine, *Story*. After his work saw a few other publications in minor literary journals, Bukowski came to the conclusion his short stories were published simply because of the fact that they were curiosity pieces. From this realization, Bukowski concluded that he would never achieve his dream of becoming a staff writer for the *Atlantic Monthly* or *Harpers,* the two major literary magazines of the time. Thus, for the next ten years Bukowski wrote little, and instead, spent his time drinking, traveling, and experiencing life.

In 1953 Bukowski was hospitalized for a bleeding ulcer. This ulcer was brought about by his excessive alcoholism and the stress caused, due to what he believed, were unbearable working conditions at the Los Angeles Post Office. Upon being released from the hospital, Bukowski again tried his hand at writing literature, which eventually proved to be his life's calling.

After a decade long exodus from attempting to find an audience for his writings, Charles Bukowski first became published as a poet in the late 1950's. As Bukowski continued to write, his poetry and prose found their way into the numerous small poetry magazines that were present during the 1950's and 1960's. During the late 1960's Bukowski wrote short stories for the *Los Angeles*

Free Press, published by Art Kunkin, which was the largest alternative newspaper in the country at that time. This exposed Bukowski's explicit style of story telling to a much larger audience. Throughout the late 1960's and into the early 1970's Bukowski additionally expanded his reader base by being published as a writer of erotica in numerous national pornography magazines.

Charles Bukowski first saw independent publication of his writings in the form of Chapbooks. Chapbook is a slang term for, "Cheap Books." Chapbooks first came into prominence in the mid 1950's as a relatively inexpensive method to publish the writings of new and budding authors. Chapbooks are generally staple bound, with a limited page count. It was Bukowski's poetry that initially found publication by this method. His first work of poetry published in this fashion occurred in 1960 with the Chapbook entitled, *Flower, Fist, and Bestial Wail.* After numerous Chapbook publications, through the decade of the 1960's, Bukowski's literature eventually found its way to national publication.

The publication of Bukowski's writings in the various literary journals, and the small independent press publication of his poetry and later his short stories and novels, moved Charles Bukowski from the status of an unknown writer, living on the fringes of society, to a literary cult icon who helped to push the boundaries of modern literature to new levels of cultural acceptance.

The literary work of Bukowski cannot be studied without the understanding that his personal view of sexuality is, no doubt, the most compelling formative topic of his literature. Bukowski explicitly detailed the exploits of his erotic encounters throughout his literary career. Bukowski's evolving understanding of sexuality will periodically be referenced in this study; therefore, his depictions of erotica must be placed into perspective in order to provide a basis for further evaluations in this study to have basis.

The blatant sexuality depicted in Bukowski's literature can be initially observed to be similar, in format, to types of sexual bragging that two young adolescent males may engage in. Bukowski's literature, however, was predominately written when he was in his late forties, onward into his seventies. Whereas, most males leave this type of boastful behavior behind with youth, Bukowski chose to embrace it throughout his literary career, thus, ultimately defining the Bukowski style of literature. An example of a typical Bukowski sexual exploit can be read in his book, *Tales of Ordinary Madness.* Bukowski writes,

> *Barney got her ass while she sucked me off; Barney finished first, put his toe in her ass, wiggled it, asked, "how ya like that?" she couldn't answer right then. she finished me off, then we drank an hour or so. then I switched to the bunghole. Barney took the mouth. after that, he went to his place, I went to mine. I drank myself to sleep.*

The obviously male orientated perspective of Bukowski's style of eroticism can be seen as the reason that men, on the whole, would be more drawn to this literature than that of women. Russell Harrison, in his essay, *Sex, Women and Irony,* defines a reason why women, generally, do not find the literature of Bukowski to be appealing. He states,

> *In his novels Bukowski has depicted a number of women through their relationships with Henry Chinaski; indeed, one of the reasons, "thoughtful female readers find no chance whatsoever to positively identify with the female characters" is that women are rarely presented independent of their relationship with Chinaski.*

From a specific frame of reference, aspects of Bukowski's writing may certainly be considered crude and pornographic. This sentiment was shared by the numerous critics who wrote critical essays on Bukowski's literature.

From his early career forward, Bukowski was often viewed by literary critics as a misogynist who possessed little respect for women. This fact was exemplified by the subject matter of which he wrote, how he approached the subject of male/female interaction, and where his early works were predominately published: namely, erotic and underground publications which sought after writings which were outside the boundaries of the common culturally accepted. An ideal example of a critic's approach to the blatant sexuality portrayed in the writings of Bukowski can be seen in the essay written by Karin Huffzky. She states,

> *In his underground society he describes a purely masculine world, in which women are hardly more than splashes of a puddle through which hardy fellows traipse, mostly*

drunk, or in which they wallow. Then
afterwards: wipe off & away! Also most of
the times drunk... almost everything in his
head is reduced to the magical actions: fuck,
drink, fight: beating women.

This perception of Bukowski's writing is
echoed by an anonymous literary critic cited in
Russell Harrison's book, *Against the American
Dream.* The critic writes,

Bukowski's antics with women, his thoughts
about them, are one vast and sniggering
cliche. He has nothing to tell us about them
and is determined at this point not to learn.
They are dirty jokes to him, a dirty joke on
him. Inside the web of his booze-bull-and
broad exploits lurks a demon sexual jingoist,
erupting and irrupting in self-punishing
concentration; hostile, frustrated,
pugilistic—fearful of the role into which (he
thinks) one is cast by fate of genitalia.

Simply reading Bukowski's literature from a
superficial perspective and labeling him as a
"Woman Hater" is not enough to truly understand
the factors which motivated Bukowski to write in
the fashion he did, for it was his explicit approach
to writing which defined and separated Bukowski
from many of his literary contemporaries. What
must be studied are the historic and personal
elements that defined Bukowski as a person, thus
giving birth to his writings. First of all, though
Bukowski began to see some of his work published
in the late 1950's and early 1960's, he did not come
to be frequently published until the mid to late

1960's. During this historical time frame in American history, free expression was embraced and was considered a human right. Thus, Bukowski was able to find a voice for his particular mindset. Had he actively sought publication for his type of literature in a previous decade, he would have, no doubt, experienced untold resistance and would have not been accepted as the literary zealot he became known as, which ultimately lead him to break new literary ground.

Russell Harrison in his essay on the early life of Bukowski helps to pinpoint many of the formative factors that led Bukowski to write about women in the fashion in which he approached the subject. Harrison states,

> *For roughly a decade, from 1945 to 1955, Bukowski published very little, indeed, nothing at all in the second half of that period. This gap has played a significant role in his career. Though born in 1920, Bukowski didn't begin to publish seriously (after a false start in the mind-1940's) until the late 1950's (his late thirties), he did not achieve significant recognition until almost a decade later and did not achieve a mastery of his medium until he was in his fifties. When this progression is combined with the fact that often enough he has taken his material (this is especially true of his novels) from the events of his childhood, youth, and early manhood, i.e., the 1920's through the 1940's, his writing can seem out of step. Hence, as is most evident in Love is a Dog from Hell (1977) and Women (1978), we have the phenomenon of a man whose*

deepest attitudes to women were shaped almost a half-century earlier than the era in which they were being given artistic expression. This had two results: first, chauvinistic traits were much more likely to be perceived as salient and to evoke stronger reaction in the context of the raised and rising consciousness of the 1970's and 1980's than even more chauvinist books of his contemporaries which had, however, been published earlier. Secondarily, the fact that Bukowski's books were being written well after the start of the women's movement meant that that movement affected them as it hadn't others.

From this analysis we see that Bukowski was more a mirror of his generation than simply that of the profound chauvinist, which was commonly depicted by many literary critics. Historically, Bukowski grew up during a period of time in the United States when women were thought of as less than men. This fact was illustrated with first-hand experience, by the young Bukowski, who witnessed the harsh treatment of his mother at the hands of his father. From these factors, Bukowski set about a life lived from the perspective of women being observed as objects, instead of as whole and complete self-worthy individuals.

When the autobiographical factors of Bukowski, as a human being, are not sufficiently taken into consideration, the previously detailed type of demeaning critical review of his writings can be seen as accurate. However, when the influential factors of his life are viewed, the subconscious source for the attitude he presented in his writings towards women may be perceived from a much different perspective. This can be substantiated by the fact that Bukowski was a man, who up until his late middle-aged life, was continually shunned by society, in no small part due to his alcoholism. The type of women Bukowski continually encountered in his drunken stupors and wanderings were generally not the type of women who were individually self-assured and self-actualized. Thus, his perception of women as lesser beings was continually reinforced from his childhood, through the period of his young adulthood, and onto his late middle age.

With these facts as a basis for understanding Bukowski's erotic twist on literature, we can view his writings from a more enlightened understanding and place them into historical and personal perspective that they deserve. The fact that many critics never looked beyond the overt sexuality portrayed by Bukowski when evaluating his work depicts how readily the commentary of the literary media can be swayed by personal tastes.

As a literary figure, Bukowski admittedly became defined and driven by the experiences of alienation that he experienced in his childhood and early adulthood. This led him down the path of alcoholism, and self-destruction. Whereas, most people who have experienced a dysfunctional childhood, and do not receive the necessary psychological counseling, continually slide further into a state of antisocial behavior, Bukowski took this seemingly misanthropic lifestyle and turned it into art. So much so, that it influenced the literature of the mid to late twentieth century.

In a letter written to Jon and Louise Webb on March 1, 1964, Bukowski ideally describes the mindset which has influenced so much of his literature.

> *I am getting a little drunk, a good wall to hide behind, the coward's flag. I remember once in some city in some cheap room, I believe it was St. Louis, yes, a hotel room on the corner and the gas fumes of traffic going to work used to come up and choke my sick lazy lungs, and I'd send her out for beer or wine and she was trying to get me straight, trying to mother me or hang me or figure me, as all women will try to do and she gave me this old bit; "Drinking is only escapism." Sure, I told her, and thank old red-balled God it is, and when I fuck you, that is escapism too, you may not think it is, to you it might be living, now let's have a drink.*

The writing of Bukowski cannot be disassociated from his life, as he writes of what he has lived and experienced. Whereas, many authors possess the ability to depict a subject they possess no personal experiential knowledge of, Bukowski, having lived on the fringes of society for so long, writes entirely from what he knows. Though not all of his works are autobiographical in nature, those that are not are stories told of individuals or situations he has personally known or witnessed. Thus, when he brings them to the first-person, it is not a life or a lifestyle far from his own. Therefore, he possesses the ability to depict them with an aura of authenticity.

Modern literature, at the time Bukowski became an active, published writer, was highly influenced by the "Beat" writers of the late 1950's and early 1960's. The "Beats" were ideally characterized by the literature of Jack Kerouac, who propagated a lifestyle defined by pursuing spiritual enlightenment and the seeking of freedom, *On the Road,* from the traditionally accepted boundaries of modern society, Bukowski's form of modern literature, however, was one of an urban dweller, continually drunk, having lurid affairs with women, and possessing an obsession for the race track. This style of literature introduced a new component to the mindset of the literary public. It allowed them to peer deeply into the mind of a man living life on the fringes of society, being controlled by the factors which dominate many people's lives; namely: the need for money, love, excitement, and acceptance.

Charles Bukowski, though defiantly not one of "The Beats," was first brought to worldwide attention by Lawrence Ferlinghetti. Ferlinghetti, a poet and author himself was deeply rooted in the "Beat" literary ideology of the 1950's. As the owner of City Lights Books, he was instrumental in bringing the works of the "Beat" poets and authors to the eyes of the world. Ferlinghetti discovered Bukowski and was the first to publish a book of his short stories on an international scale. Neeli Cherkovski biography, Ferlinghetti describes,

> *In 1972, Ferlinghetti brought out Erections, Ejaculations, Exhibitions, and General Tales of Ordinary Madness by Charles Bukowski, a collection of short stories edited by Gail Chiarrello. The stories had appeared in various underground magazines and newspapers over the years and had gained there for their author a large*

following, Bukowski first came to Ferlinghetti's attention for his poetry, published widely in the small literary magazines throughout the sixties. He saw immediately that Bukowski's fiction was a natural for City Lights. Bukowski's stories were set mostly in Los Angeles, and related the author's crazy exploits in the proletarian world of racetrack, odd jobs, booze, and low life. Ferlinghetti saw Bukowski as the single most important prose writer of the period and accurately predicted his rising popularity with reader and critics alike. Soon Notes of a Dirty Old Man was added to the City Lights list, and Ferlinghetti would have published an endless number of his books; however, Bukowski remained loyal to John Martin of Black Sparrow, who had published his poems and had long been a supporter and friend.

The most interesting and almost ironic fact about Ferlinghetti discovering and publishing Bukowski, is that Bukowski was never a fan of "Beat" poetry or literature. Referenced in several of his poems and his prose is the fact that he thought very little of "The Beats" as a literary group. Bukowski writes,

they hang in the parks with the Che idol, with pictures of Castro in their amulets, going OOOOOOOOMMMMM OOOOOOOMMM while William Burroughs, Jean Genet and Allen Ginsberg lead them. these writers have gone, soft, cuckoo, eggshit, female—not homo but female—and if I were a cop I'd feel like clubbing their addled brains myself. hang me for that. the writer of the streets is getting his soul cock-sucked by the idiots. there is only one place to write and that is ALONE at a typewriter. a writer who has to go into the streets is a writer who does not know the streets. I have seen enough factories, whorehouses, jails, bars, park orators to last 100 men 100 lifetimes.

From this description of three of the primary "Beat" literary figures, we come to understand that Bukowski actually looked down upon their method of writing and their approach to life. He felt that they did not possess a true understanding of the street life that they often wrote about. In fact, we can conclude that Bukowski felt their literary methods and their technique were invalid. Certainly Bukowski had the ability to view any writer, as he deemed appropriate, due to his own individual psychological and artistic understandings. The most interesting fact about the above passage, however, is that Ferlinghetti published this critical review of "Beat" authors in Bukowski's book, published by City Lights, *Notes of a Dirty Old Man.* Ferlinghetti published this work notwithstanding the fact that he possessed long-standing relationships with the above-mentioned authors. Thus, it was to Ferlinghetti's credit that he was so enamored by the writing style of Bukowski that he did not let it cloud his appraisal of his work or cause him to invoke his editorial powers in the rewording of any of Bukowski's ideologies.

Neeli Cherkovski in his book, *Hank: The Life of Charles Bukowski* elaborates on the mindset of Bukowski in regards to the "Beats." He writes,

> *He read Allen Ginsberg's Howl and Gregory Corso's poetry, like many other poets writing for the small journals or "littles," as he called them, but he was unimpressed. What annoyed him most about the Beat poets was their engagement in social and political issues. He believed this hampered their poetry, that a pure poet had greater concerns than tampering with current affairs.*

Bukowski's method of literature was to take the reader deeply into a life situation and slap them in the face with it. There is never the ideology conveyed that life would all be better if a different set of redefined circumstances were present; nor does he concede that through some mystical approach the general perception of life will be enhanced. What Bukowski writes about is exacting, blatant, and self-revealing issues. From this style of literature, he takes the reader deeply into his own mindset and the intimate factors of described interrelationships that personally affect him. He writes,

> *Bukowski cried when Judy Garland sang at the N.Y. Philharmonic, Bukowski cried when Shirley Temple sang "I Got Animal Crackers in my Soup;" Bukowski cried in cheap flophouses, Bukowski can't dress, Bukowski can't talk, Bukowski is scared of women, Bukowski has a bad stomach,*

Bukowski is full of fears and hates dictionaries, nuns, pennies, busses, churches, park benches, spiders, flies, fleas, freaks; Bukowski didn't go to war. Bukowski is old, Bukowski hasn't flown a kite for 45 years; if Bukowski were an ape they'd run him out of the tribe.

As demonstrated, Bukowski writes from a purely emotional frame of reference. The tales, often times depicted in an almost poetic fashion, invoke a response in the reader that goes beyond the simple telling of a story.

Erections, Ejaculation, and General Tales of Ordinary Madness, published by City Lights Books in 1972 was made up of sixty-eight short stories authored by Charles Bukowski. The material that made up this book was, in 1983, separated in order to form two individual volumes, *Tales of Ordinary Madness* and *The Most Beautiful Woman in Town and Other Stories.* In each of the short stories which make up this collection, the reader is allowed to not only view various elements of what may be defined as, "The Bukowski's Style of Literature," but is equally allowed to view elements of Bukowski's personal life experience.

the kid and I were the last of a drunken party at my place, and we were sitting there when somebody outside began blowing a car horn, loud LOUD LOUD it was, oh sing loude, but then everything is axed through the head anyway. the world is done, so I sat there with my drink, smoking a cigar, thinking of nothing—the poets were gone,

85

the poets with the ladies were gone, it was
fairly pleasant even with the horn going.

Idealized in this story is the lifestyle that
Bukowski lived during the mid to late 1960's. He
was in a continual state of inebriation, whenever he
was not working at the Post Office, which at this
point in his life had been his job for nearly a decade,
until 1970 when he finally quit. His associations
were predominantly with others of the Los Angeles
poetry and literary community. Thus, many of his
tales were based on interactions with these people.
"The Kid" he refers to in this story is the eventual
author of Bukowski's and Ferlinghetti's biography,
Neeli Cherkovski; known, at that time, under the
pen name, Neeli Cherry.

Bukowski's desired meditative-like state of
intoxication can be duly witnessed in this opening
passage to this story entitled, *Night Streets of
Madness.* He sits with his drink and his cigar in the
mind state of nothingness.

Bukowski had the ability to present his
drunkenness in this Zen like fashion, making it
similar to details of meditation described by the sect
of yogis in India who follow the path to *Samadhi*
(enlightenment) by partaking of *Ganja.* In this yogi
sect, they utilize hashish and then enter into a drug-
induced state of meditation upon their chosen deity,
generally Shiva or Kali. They claim enlightened
visions and a perpetual state of divine nothingness,
not dissimilar to Bukowski's. The horn was
honking, yet he was free of this worldly distraction.

*"listen," said the kid, "let's go out there and
tell them to fuck-off. tell him to jam that
horn up his ass." the kid wasn't a bad*

writer, and he had the ability to laugh at himself, which is sometimes a sign of greatness, or at least a sign that you have the chance to end up being something else besides a stuffed literary turd. the world was full of stuffed literary turds talking about the time they met Pound at Spoleto or Edmund Wilson in Boston or Dali in his underwear.

Bukowski was admittedly one of those who wrote and embraced the literary world. Yet, as can be easily witnessed in his previous passage, he had a distaste for all of those who walked the peripheries of the arts and attempted to associate with those like himself, who lived the creative path. Throughout all of Bukowski's literature, he continually takes aim at those who follow this path. As time went by and his fame increased, he too found large groups of peoples attempting to associate with him, solely for the reason of interacting with a seemingly famous literary figure.

As we look at the one time shunned young boy and young man, we see that though he would later make disenfranchising comments about these people in his writings, he still, none-the-less, allowed them to continually be in his presence. From this, Bukowski in his early years of notoriety, no doubt, gained much of the needed affection and sense of belonging that was absent from his early life.

"let's go out there and tell them to jam that horn up their ass," said the kid, influenced by the Bukowski myth (I am really a coward).

Throughout the early years of Bukowski published writings he would often refer to the, "Tough Guy Drunkard Bukowski Myth." Almost as if to create it, focus on it, and to make it more widespread, he continually referred to this fact. In addition to these statements, he often would write of his impending fame and published notoriety. In an effort to self publicize, there seems to be no better vehicle than Bukowski's own work about himself.

Bukowski, when depicting the erotic in his literature was often times very blatant in his writing. He writes,

> *I went into the bedroom and got into bed with Jeanie, she was a large woman, and naked. I began kissing her breasts, sucking at them. "hey what are you doing?" "doin? I'm going to fuck you!" I put my finger into her cunt and moved it back and forth.*

There can be seen two direct sources of inspiration for this type of erotic literary style; the first is the blatantly misogynistic expectations of the pornographic journals Bukowski wrote for, the second is his life long sense of insecurity, developed in his childhood. These two factors in association with the literary freedom and the disrespect for accepted society commonly propagated in the 1960's allowed for this type of literature to be viewed in a new and dramatically different literary context. In the 1960's it could be seen as a work of descriptive art. At an earlier time, it would have been viewed as pornography.

With this freedom of expression as a basis, Bukowski was allowed to move forward, redefining the realms of bohemian literature, taking it to the level where sexually dominated situations were clearly spelled out. This is in stark contrast to the aforementioned work of Jack Kerouac, who during the late 1950's and early 1960's would imply that sexual activity took place in his novels, but would never come out and acutely detail the occurrences.

> *I mounted and then very SLOWLY SLOWLY QUIETLY so the springs would not rattle, so there would not be a sound, I slid it in and out in and out EVER SO SLOWLY and when I came I thought I would never stop. it was one of the best fucks of my life, as I wiped off on the sheets the thought occurred to me—it could be that Man has been fucking improperly for centuries.*

Brazen in his approach to his sexuality, and defiantly written from a male perspective, Bukowski had the ability, none-the-less, in allowing the wording he used to describe sexual activity to end in a poetic fashion, describing the unthought of or the unexpected. As each individual possesses a particular predetermined mind frame to each occurrence in his life, and each individual attributes a specific set of standards to each experience, Bukowski, possessed the ability to take the obvious and move it to a literary level where the mind of the reader is forced to view the situation from a new and different perspective. Thus, this became much of the basis of Bukowski's literary style.

Bukowski would comment on this book (in its combined state), in a letter to Carl Weisner in February of 1972,

I'll try to get the City Lights book to you when It comes out. I do think the stories fouler (better) than Notes of a D.O. Man. Instead of calling it Bukowskiana (not my idea), I have retitled it Erections, Ejaculations, Exhibitions, and General Tales of Ordinary Madness. At the printer's now, say L.F. He calls it a great book. I agree. I don't think that since Artaud or Nietzsche there has been anybody as joyfully mad as I am well.

The back cover to the City Lights Edition of *Notes of a Dirty Old Man,* written by Ferlinghetti, reads,

These stories originally published by Essex House have become unavailable to both general readers and the readers of unusual literature. CITY LIGHTS has rescued them from their hidden immortality with this new edition. It's Bukowski again—mad drunk, wounded, screaming, starving, wondering, feeling it out in his rough, raw style. Buk is a true descendant of Artaud Celine and F. Dos. For those who prefer the fact to the fiction, here is an almost-diary of the trapped man, trapped in a society that only gives credence to the unreal and the useless. Bukowski's farts are realer than the Empire State Building, and his loves and hates come out dancing, clothed in a gentle humor which is the difference between self-pity and great art. For those who enjoyed his ERECTIONS, EJACULATIONS,

EXHIBITIONS AND GENERAL TALES OF ORDINARY MADNESS here also are some pure inventive tales, but again touched by Buk's rawness and his screams and his laughter. Charley's genius is his ability to pass his feelings down through the line into the reader (an almost direct contact as if the pages themselves breathed and moved). Here is the warmth and the rage of the writer-poet who has caused more reaction and counter-reaction than anybody who has arrived in the last decade. He is cursed with a demented power. Read him and vote.

Ferlinghetti and City Lights Books in their obvious attempt to publicize and sell this book of short stories aptly describes in a few artistically concocted, sales orientated, words the life of Bukowski. In doing so, they depict the Bukowski myth and, thus, not only enhance it but unleash it to the uninitiated.

As is often the case with published literary figures, Bukowski was presented as the artist who lived outside of the societal norm. This allowed others who lived this lifestyle to relate to him and those who live within society's bounds to idealize him. City Lights never referred to the fact that Bukowski, during this period of time, had a long-standing job at the post office, in order that his artistic myth could be further extended.

The back cover "Author Description" utilized by City Lights is just the type of sales pitch which Bukowski would have written for himself, had he been given the chance, as can be witnessed in his numerous own self depictions in his poetry and literature. Additionally, Artaud and Celine were two of the few authors Bukowski appreciated, as can be witness in a letter he wrote to Joseph Conte on June 27, 1966. In it he states,

> *Artaud one of the few writers I look up to. Artaud, Dostoevsky, Celine... read Celine, Joe, this guy was laughing while they were killing him.*

Therefore, his being mentioned in the same category as the previous two authors would have obviously pleased the aging Bukowski.

In *Notes of a Dirty Old Man*, which was originally published in 1969 by a small press and then assigned for republication by City Lights Books in 1973, Bukowski tells an array of stories, lived through personal experiences. In the opening tale he writes,

> *but she was a big white woman and she went for these Filipinos, the Filipinos did tricks man, things no white man would ever dream of, even me: these Flips are gone now with their George Raft pulldown widebrims and padded-shoulders; they used to be the fashion leaders, the stiletto boys; leather heels, greasy evil faces—where have you gone?*

This segment is initially interesting in terms of literary styling due to the fact of what was considered "Politically Correct" and acceptable at the time when this book was first published in 1969, and then republished in 1973 by City Lights. For here we see that Bukowski was allowed to refer to an ethnic minority by what would be, by today's standards, considered a racial slur. Certainly, racially derogatory comments are made all of the time by groups of all racially homogeneous peoples. None-the-less, this type of comment, in a literary sense, would more aptly than not be removed by a publisher in our current period of time, twenty-five years later. This is especially the case as the term "Flip" served no purpose to the overall trend of the storyline, except to view how, Bukowski, himself titled this race of people in his mind.

From another perspective we could view the previous passage as Bukowski associating his character with the way in which the average Caucasian person of the time period witnessed and delineated the Filipino male. In fact, the terms he used may simply have been considered appropriate or, in fact, a product of "Hip Culture" during the 1940's. In any case, racial descriptive words such as, "Flip" are illustrative of a time gone by in literary publications.

In viewing the literary motivational factors Bukowski possessed at this period of his life, we find that, here again, Bukowski goes back to the type of social behavior learned in his dysfunctional childhood. He was called ethnically based derogatory names due to his being from Germany; thus, he learned at a young age that this type of behavior was acceptable and socially normal.

Beyond the obvious implications of this wording, the reader is allowed to see deeply into the mind of Bukowski with this passage. Though the title, "Flip" possesses obvious racially negative connotations, it is obvious he possessed a certain reverence for their style and a certain longing for the outward expression of the style they possessed to once again be prevalent. From this, the reader comes to understand that though seemingly negative racial connotations are used to depict people of a specific ethnic background, in the mind of the author, lies a deeper understanding of the differences people possess. Thus, the term "Flip" set about a thought process initially in the mind of Bukowski and later in that of the reader, that the Filipino men of a certain period of time were creative lovers and followed a fashionable pattern of stylish dressing. The conclusion which can be reached from this is that titles, be they positive or negative, are simply the depiction of an image to the mind of the individual, and thus, the word used should not be thought to truly possess either a positive or negative quality. Instead, it should be viewed simply as what it is, a word which conjures up visual images to the mind of the individual

The short story, of which this segment was a part, is told of how the night before Bukowski had gotten into a fight with a man in his rooming house, with whom he was gambling. In the fight, they had destroyed Bukowski's room. Thus, he had to wait until it was night to sneak out to avoid paying the charges for the wrecked furniture. When nighttime came, he planned his escape.

> I opened the door a bit, chain still on, and there was one, a little Flip monkey with a hammer. When I opened the door, he lifted the hammer and grinned. when I closed the door he took the tacks out of his mouth and pretended to pound them into the rug of the stairway leading to the first floor and the only door out. I'd open the door he'd lift the hammer and grin. Shit monkey!

The obvious signs of constant paranoia, another signature of Bukowski literature, are well written into this piece. Bukowski believes that the man is waiting for him to leave the room, with the hope of somehow making him pay for damages rendered. Finally Bukowski leaves,

> *HEY! WHERE YOU GO? the little monkey began to rise to one knee, he raised the hammer, and that's all I needed—the flash of electric light on the hammer—I had the suitcase in the left hand, the portable steel typer in the right, he was in perfect position, down by my knee and I swung with great accuracy and some anger, I gave him the flat and heavy and hard side, greatly, long the side of his head, his skull, his temple, his being.*

After a cab ride Bukowski finds himself at Union Station waiting for a bus.

> *I sat in the bus depot for an hour waiting for the bus to New Orleans, wondering if I had killed the guy. I finally got on with typewriter and suitcase, jamming typewriter far into the overhead rack, not wanting the thing to fall on my head. it was a long ride with much drinking and some involvement with a redhead from Fort Worth. I got off at Fort Worth too, but she lived with her mother and I had to get a room, and I got a room in a whorehouse by mistake. all night the women hollering things like "HEY! you're not going to stick THAT thing in ME for ANY kind of money!" toilets flushing all*

*night, doors opening and closing. the
redhead, she was a nice innocent thing, or
bargained for a better man. anyhow, I left
town without getting into her pants. I finally
made it to New Orleans.*

The story proceeds and illustrates how
Bukowski possessed the ability, in a very few
words, to change story focus and train of thought.
This is no doubt due to the freedom of quick
expression he learned from his years of writing
poetry. In almost a free flowing fashion, Bukowski
can change subject matter to continue the story
without the need for unnecessary wording and
burdensome details. Again, Bukowski embraces a
Zen-like freedom in his movement with his
literature—it moves forward but is not bound by
commonly accepted form.

In terms of functional grammatical styling,
we witness that in several, but not all, of the stories
which make up *Tales of Ordinary Madness* and *The
Most Beautiful Women in Town and Other Stories,*
and *Notes of a Dirty Old Man,* a capital letter is not
used in association with the opening of a sentence.
This minor literary detail can be seen as a stylistic
convention of an era, the 1960's, when artists and
authors intentionally choose to make obvious
statements against the commonly accepted norm.
Bukowski, obviously was not above this type of a
statement. He did not, however, use the small "i" as
was the case of, E.E. Cummings, thus, any sentence
which began with "I" began with a capital letter.

Bukowski believed his disassociation from
accepted grammatical rules to be a statement of
literary freedom. This in association with his free
flowing patterns of story structure and construction

allowed him to create novels without being bound by the rules traditionally associated with precisely written literary works commonly accepted at this period of time. Critics, however, did not always believe that Bukowski's lack of literary structure to be, in fact, a study in art, as opposed to simply being sloppy writing technique. This can be witnessed in the critique written by Julian Smith on, *Notes of a Dirty Old Man,* published by City Lights Books. He states,

> *A deliberately disorderly syntax, a "spontaneous" typewritten verse that creates its effect by a radical difference from smoother, more literary writing... Bukowski flavors the lexical stew of Notes with misspellings, ungrammatical construction, sentences with no verbs, repetitions, split infinitives, much slang and swearing, sexual innuendo and other linguistic ambiguities that enable him to splice sexuality, violence, nastiness and humor. By deliberating leaving in the text the sort of grammatical confusions common in speech but usually suppressed in written English, Bukowski is indicating that he wants to align writing with spoken rather than written conventions.*

This stylistic function was lost quickly once Bukowski's short stories and later full novels were published predominately by Black Sparrow Press. Black Sparrow Press was created, owned, and its early editions edited by John Martin.

Martin was, a serious, soft-spoken man, he never played into the Bukowski myth. Martin, in fact, was a Straight laced, church-going man, neither a drinker nor a smoker, who lived a sedate, comfortable family life,

details Neeli Cherkovski in his biography *Hank.*

Martin, was a well-read man, and took Bukowski's literary talent especially, initially, in terms of his poetry very seriously. Martin's Black Sparrow Press initially published Bukowski's poetry, thus, exposing him to the likes of Ferlinghetti. Cherkovski continues,

John Martin edited and published a collection of Bukowski's short stories, work that had not gone into the City Lights collection, and some newer stories, under the title, South of No North. The subtitle, Stories of the Buried Life, is a revelatory footnote to how the writer viewed himself during much of his life. There are twenty-seven stories in the collection, including All the Assholes in the World and Mine and Confessions of a Man Insane Enough To Live With Beasts.

South Of No North takes the reader through a combination of Bukowski's early literary stylings. At times the stories are set in the first-person and at other times they are told in the narrative. At the heart of every tale told is a man on the outskirts of society attempting to forge a place for himself in an unaccepting world.

Love and lust are central to the storyline of several of the short stories that make up this book, as is often the case in Bukowski literature. Bukowski writes in the narrative,

> *Yet a man needed a woman now and then, if for no other reason than to prove he could get one. The sex was secondary. It wasn't a lover's world, it never would be.*

From here we see his resistance to the desire of long lasting love and deeply rooted affection. Relationships were merely a subject that provided an individual a confirmation of his manhood, his ability to reach out, make contact, prove he was whole, and then return to the shell of which he lived prior to the experience. This was not dissimilar from the relationships Bukowski found as he roamed the country in his early years; they were as transient as he, himself, was.

One of the most telling of short stories in this book is that of *A Shipping Clerk With a Red Nose*. In this work, Bukowski tells the story of himself coming into his own early notoriety. He does this artistically from the first-person standpoint of a small poetry magazine editor who visits him in search of poetry. The illustrative words Bukowski chooses to describe himself delineates how he saw himself as unattractive and unlovable, depictions which follow him throughout all the years of his literary work.

> *Randal was known as an isolationist, a drunk, a crude and bitter man but his poems were raw, raw and honest, simple and*

savage. He was writing unlike anybody else at the time.

Here the reader clearly sees that though Bukowski saw himself and described himself as an outcast from society, he believed, rightly so, that his poetry was a new symbol of a changing society.

Bukowski, as a human being, can never be psychologically separated from his work, as his life lead a path of obviously accepted psychological and cultural abnormality. It is interesting how he viewed his work, however, seeing it as a "Cut Above," when he proudly describes himself as antisocial. From this can be concluded two factors, both based in psychological understanding. The first is that, as he could not love himself, he found an object, his created work, to focus his affections upon. Second, as he received no approval from any other area of his life, poetry and literature was his only method of self gratification and proved that he was more than the nothing he had come to define himself as.

This type of literary self-debasing that Bukowski employed was not limited to a single story. In fact, he employed it several times. In the short story *Dr. Nazi,* Bukowski begins,

> *Now, I'm a man of many problems and I suppose that most of them are self-created. I mean with a female, and the gambling, and feeling hostile towards groups of people, and the larger the group, the greater the hostility. I'm called negative and gloomy, sullen. I keep remembering the female who screamed at me: "You're so god damned negative! Life can be beautiful!" I suppose it*

can, and especially with a little less screaming.

Bukowski was not oblivious to his psychological situation. In fact, he marveled in it and attached humor to the subject. We find a man, in Bukowski, who again embraced a seemingly Zen acceptance of his fate. He observed it, witnessed it, took notice of it, and accepted the fact it was the way it was. A more self-actualized individual may have attempted a change in his social skills, but by this point in Bukowski's life, particularly in his poetry, this was who he was. He possessed a reason to remain constant in his emotional state. Had the poetry not been published, would he have been so adamant? Of course, this is a philosophic question, not based in fact, but he probably would have simply followed the path of alcoholism and racetrack gambling that defined his life. The published poetry and short stories simply gave him more reason to be the outsider, the hater of society and people on the whole which he purported to be.

Bukowski's poetry is multitudinous. Poetry was obviously Bukowski's first love, due to the simplistic nature of its creation, he could simply live an experience and place it upon paper. Though it was first his short stories which brought Bukowski's literature to the eyes of the world, from 1969 forward with the publication of, *The Days Run Away Like Wild Horse Over the Hills,* by Black Sparrow Press, Bukowski's poetic license etched its way across the page, interrupting the path of the traditionally accepted subject matter and verse of conventional poetics.

Bukowski's focus, in his poetry, was never solely on females or sexuality. In fact, his poetry found its way to this subject matter far less than did his short stories. Bukowski's poetry focused much more profoundly on the explicit derailings of a man witnessing the world from the outside, an individual who is never allowed true passage into friendship or acceptance.

Bukowski writes his poetry predominately from the first-person perspective, detailing the experiences he has in life, from his own unique, highly personally analytical, perspective. He approached his writing almost as a cultural historian or sociological researcher would, as he precisely details the physical, cultural, and moral norms of many of the situations he encounters. This can be illustrated by his opening passage of his poem *One For Ging, With Klux Top,*

> *I live among rats and roaches*
> *but there is this highrise apt., a new one*
> *across from me, glimmering pool, lived in*
> *by very young*
> *people with new cars, mostly red or white*
> *cars,*
> *and I allow myself to look upon the scene as*
> *some type of miracle world*
> *not because it is possibly so*
> *but because it is easier to think this way,*
> *- why take more knives? -*
> *so today I sat here and I saw one young man*
> *sitting in his red car*
> *sucking his thumb and waiting*
> *as another young man, obviously a friend,*
> *talked to a young woman dressed in kind of*
> *long slim short*
> *pants, yes, and a black ill-fitting blouse,*
> *and she had on some kind of high-pointed*

hat, rather
like the kukluxklan wears, and the other
young man sucked, sat and
sucked his thumb
in the
red car and
behind them, through the glass door
the other young people sat and sat and sat
and sat around the blue pool.

In this work of prose, we see Bukowski precisely detailing the urban geographical and social class structure of late 1960's Hollywood, California. During this period of Hollywood history, the city saw a vast new influx of young people relocating from many locations around the United States. With this population movement came the construction of many new, multi-unit, apartment buildings for these new, predominately young, arrivals to inhabit. These structures were in sharp contrast to the existing housing which had been built pre-1940's. Bukowski with his own unique style of observation details this occurrence from the perspective of a man witnessing this new insurgence and being in some ways envious of the financial holdings these young people possessed. Here again, Bukowski, from the positioning of an outsider, was left viewing a world he could not help but be desirous of.

Bukowski's poetic depictions in his early-published poetry were not limited to the desirous prose of a man who did not fit in. In the second book of poetry, published by Black Sparrow Press in 1972, *Mockingbird Wish Me Luck,* Bukowski writes of his life experiences on the dark side of the city of Los Angeles.

Bartenders are human too
and when he reached for the baseball bat
the little Italian hit him in the face
with a bottle
and several whores screamed.
I was just coming out
of the men's room
when I saw the bartender
get off the floor
and open the cigar box
to get the gun,
and I turned around
and went back,
and the Italian
must have argued poorly
because I heard the shot
just as I got
the car door open.

In this poem we see that not only does Bukowski detail the violent down side of the urban environment which he inhabits, but he also gives the reader a very astute look into the social strata of the "low-life" bar scene of Los Angeles, where fatal violence was not unheard of. Bukowski continually references his own personal experiences in all of his literary works. He never attempts to step beyond the realms of his own personal knowledge. From this, the reader not only gets a clear view of a specific aspect of the lower class urban lifestyle of Los Angeles but additionally a very defined view into the way Bukowski perceived society.

Bukowski wrote poetry about the physical and psychological experiences he encounters from his own level of perception. This is common with all authors. Bukowski, in his writings, would turn the course of certain events to culminate in the way he perceived they should have ended or in the way in which he wished they had concluded, in order that his poems and short stories would possess more shock value. The periodic consistency of this artistic license can only be speculated upon. This evidence that it did, in fact, occur can be substantiated in the book written by California State University, Long Beach professor, Gerald Locklin, *Charles Bukowski: A Sure Bet.* In this book Locklin describes just such a circumstance at a reading Bukowski was giving to one of the professor's classes.

> *I'd warned him that some students would probably have to leave during the reading for classes, and one heavy door did slam fairly loudly when a young lady let it swing shut by itself. Bukowski wrote a poem alleging that she had stormed out in a huff.*

Through this method of story telling some historical facts may be altered, the actual works themselves, none-the-less, remain constant as a depiction of the mind of Charles Bukowski. Thus, the reader is allowed to come to understand the mind of the man if not the actual occurrences he depicts.

Bukowski during his early period of poetics did not always focus upon the seemingly factual. He would, at times, veer into the abstract. For example in his poem, *life,* he writes,

> *to be eaten by a hog with*
> *bad breath*
> *a the lemon swings in the wind*

yellow and ours.

This virtual haiku type poem can be seen as a response to the era in which it was created, a time in the late 1960's and early 1970's when the abstraction of Zen, commonly associated with the use of hallucinogenic drugs in the Unites States, brought about this type of response to the common cultural acceptance of a concrete and defined world. The creating of this type of poem illustrates that Bukowski was not oblivious to eternal influences, even at this stage of his life. Though his later poetry never again reflected this type of external influence, his creation of this poem does illustrate how Bukowski possessed the ability to take the abstract and move it into an arena of writing where he felt more comfortable, "to be eaten by a hog with bad breath..."

It was often written by critics and discussed among the reading literary masses that Bukowski's poetry changed during the late 1960's and early 1970's. Bukowski, himself, writes about this fact in his short story, *Goodbye Watson.*

> *Who was it? Charles Bukowski. Who's that? A poet. He's slipped. He can't write as well as he used o. But he used to wrote some great stuff. Poems of loneliness. He's really a very lonely fellow but he doesn't know it.*
> *As in all cases, personal appetites define tastes. This too was the case with the poetry of Bukowski.*

As the 1970's came upon Bukowski, not only did fifteen years of serious writing come to define his approach to the composition of his poetry

106

but also in addition he came to find a voice, an audience, and group of admirers who chose to associate with him, if for no other reason than the fact he was a published author. This, in association with the changing mindset of the 1970's, focusing less upon the abstract and more upon the concrete, guided Bukowski away from the abstraction we found in his previously detailed poem, life, and caused him to write about his life experiences in a more uniform, realistic fashion. Certainly, Bukowski still allowed his poetry to move beyond commonly accepted topics and push the boundaries of language by conveying his message in an artistic fashion, but the 1970's saw him veer away from the occasional transcendentally structured poem and focus more upon the unfeigned.

Bukowski's poetry was not always composed in the style of singular line, free verse. Often times his prose took on the form of what may have been seen as possessing structural similarities to a short story, even if the content was less delineated. An example of this can be witnessed in the poem, *john dillinger and le chasseur maudit,* in the collection, *Burning in Water Drowning in Flame.* He writes,

> *it's unfortunate, and simply not the style, but*
> *I don't care: girls remind me of hair in the*
> *sink, girls remind me of intestines and*
> *bladders and excretory movements; it's*
> *unfortunate also that ice-cream ells, babies,*
> *engine-valves, lagiostomes, palm trees,*
> *footsteps in the hall... all excite me with the*
> *cold calmness of he gravestone, nowhere,*
> *perhaps, is there sanctuary except in*
> *hearing that there were other desperate*

men: Dillinger, Rimbaud, Villon, Babyface
Nelson, Seneca, Van Gogh.

Bukowski's books of poetry collections
were always punctuated with novels and collections
of short stories. From this, his audience came to
view two sides of his literary talent.

Post Office was the first formal novel
written by Bukowski. It tells the tale of his path to
his first marriage, his fatherhood, his eventual
employment at the post office, and the exploits of
his life that took place while he was employed
there.

Bukowski wrote a letter to Carl Weissner,
his German confidant who helped to launch his
career in that country, on July 23, 1970, concerning
the oncoming publication of Post Office.

> Yes Martin has me worried. I'd prefer Post
> Office in its original raw form. of course, I
> was a little bit out of my head when I wrote
> it, but it wasn't sloppy or lazy writing; it
> was written as it fucking well came out, and
> that meant turds and blood and the rest of
> the wash. I'm told parts of it are in the
> present tense and parts are in the past.
> that's all right with me. I know most of the
> rules of grammar but I'm not interested. he
> has inferred that he doesn't want to detract
> from my style, so there we are on the merry-
> go-round. he's a nice guy but he does treat
> me too much like an idiot. he admits I'm his
> best seller but at the same time he'd rather I
> wrote more safe shit.

Here we see that in the process of literary achievement, often times, elements of an author's personal style are overlooked. This fact is generally in the hands of the editor, who changes and rearranges the material to the degree where he believes it will be considered acceptable to the grammatically educated masses. This can first be seen in the Bukowski work published by Black Sparrow where all the sentences beginning with small letters were alleviated. It is, in fact, somewhat sad to know that this process of extensive reedits took place to the works of Charles Bukowski, as it can only be imagined what new literary ground might have been expanded upon if this had not been the case.

Bukowski, during the process of composing this, his first, novel, was continually side tracked by a continuum of friends and fans who would show up at his apartment in East Hollywood to get intoxicated with him. Thus, the actual creation of the work took much longer to get started than his publisher, John Martin had hoped. Finally, Bukowski got to work on it. In his later novel, Women, there are references to the process of creating this, his first novel. In addition to this description of his writing *Post Office*, he refers to his second and final wife, Lyndia, (Linda King). A woman he met during the composition of this book.

I'm not sure when I first saw Lyndia Vance. It was about 6 Years ago and I had just quit a twelve year job as a postal clerk and was trying to be a writer. I was terrified and drank more than ever. I was attempting my first novel. I drank a pint of whiskey and two six packs of beer each night while writing. I smoked cheap cigars and typed and drank and listened to classical music on the radio until dawn. I set a goal of ten pages a night while writing. I'd get up in the morning, vomit, then walk to the front room and look on the couch to see how many pages were there. I always exceeded my ten. Sometimes there were 17, 18, 23, 25 pages. Of course, the work of each night had to be cleaned up or thrown away. It took me twenty-one nights to write my first novel.

It is interesting to note that this novel, in its original form, is made up of only one hundred and fifteen pages, of which approximately ten are re-typings of letters the post office sent to him complaining of his tardiness and bad work habits. Thus, by comparison to his other works this novel is one of Bukowski's shortest in overall page count.

Post Office, though a novel, is composed of numerous, very short chapters. These chapters are written in the very quick, free form fashion that made up Bukowski's books of short stories. In essence, very little changed in style or form between this novel and his short story collections.

Bukowski, in this novel, initially tells the tale of how his first interaction with the Post Office came about as a result of a Christmas season mail deliveryman's temporary employment.

It was Christmas season and I learned from the drunk up on the hill, who did the trick every Christmas, that they would hire damned near anybody, and so I went and the next thing I knew I had this leather sack on my back and I was hiking around at my leisure. What a job, I thought. Soft! They only gave you a block or 2.

This job was temporary and soon Bukowski was back to his hard drinking and making money at various odd jobs and at the racetrack. It wasn't until the birth of his daughter, Marina, when he was directed to obtain full time employment.

> *"Hank I can't stand it!"*
> *"You can't stand what baby?"*
> *"The situation."*
> *"What situation, babe?"*
> *"Me working and you laying around. All the neighbors think I am supporting you."*
> *"Hell, I worked and you laid around"*
> *"That's different. You're a man, I'm a woman."*
> *"Oh, I didn't know that. I thought you bitches were always screaming of equal rights?"*

With this, Bukowski found himself employed back at the Post Office. This was, obviously, a position that existed in association with numerous employment problems for the next ten years. Bukowski was driven to this employment by the fact that though his poetry, short stories, and late books were selling, they were not making him enough money to survive and pay the child support for his daughter, as his wife eventually left him.

Through the novel, Bukowski makes references to the racetrack and how, at times, he had developed a system that allowed him to win; systems that he believed would never desert him. In each case they always did, however, and he would return to employment at the Post Office. The exploits that occurred in reference to the racetrack are, no doubt, the most moving of the novels. Bukowski writes,

> *One day I was at the bar between races and I saw   this woman. God or somebody keeps creating women and tossing them out on the streets, and this one's ass is too big and that one's tits are to small and this one is mad and that one is crazy and that one is a religionist and that one reads tea leaves and this one can't control her farts, and that one has this big nose, and that one had boney legs...   But now and then, a woman walks up, full blossom, a woman just bursting from her dress...a sex creature, a curse, the end of it all. I looked up and there she was, down at the end of the bar. She was about drunk and the bar tender wouldn't serve her.*

As previously discussed, Bukowski possessed an unequaled ability to rapidly define a situation, outline its context, and then move quickly into storyline all within a few sentences. In the preceding segment we come to clearly understand this process as Bukowski took his love for the racetrack, his continual flirtation with drink, his ideology towards women, and the meeting of a female which he found appropriate and economically placed all of this random information into a few well chosen sentences.

Bukowski possessed the ability to make his individual life philosophies and chosen desires into literary art, as opposed to simply mentally pondering the rambling obsessive thoughts of a drunkard. He did this by making his observations elemental to the storyline, as can be witnessed in the previous paragraph. Bukowski never personally discussed whether this literary ability was a byproduct of his ongoing alcoholism or was a clearly refined practice of authorship. The causation factor can be speculated upon, as his alcoholism, no doubt, caused him to overlook many of the literary rules practiced by other authors of his time. Thus, he was not bound by formalities and could compose literature from a mindset of freedom. Bukowski, with his free flowing style of writing, was able to redefine the art of literature and allowed the ideology of a drunkard to be raised to the level of true art.

Bukowski continually wrote, during this period of his career, as if he were personally telling a story to a single individual in close proximity to himself. This technique draws the reader into an intimate relationship with the first-person Bukowski and the other characters he portrays in his writing. This style of composition allows the reader to feel close to him and empathize with his life situation.

Bukowski goes on in telling the tale of his meeting with the previously discussed woman. He writes,

> *We drank the rest of the card. She brought me luck. I hit two of the last three. "Did you bring a car?" I asked her. "I came with some damn fool," she said. "Forget him." "If you can I can," I told her. We wrapped up in the car and her tongue flicked in and out of my mouth like a tiny lost snake. We unwrapped and I drove down the coast. It was a lucky night. I got a table overlooking*

the ocean and we ordered drinks and waited
for the steaks. Everybody in the place looked
at her. I leaned forward and lit her
cigarette, thinking, this one's going to be a
good one. Everybody in the place knew what
I was thinking and Mary Lou knew what I
was thinking, and I smiled at her over the
flame.

In the preceding passage we see how Bukowski was constantly aware of thoughts of the people around him, or at least what he believed them to be thinking. From this, we are again lead into the paranoiac mindset of Bukowski the individual. Whereas most authors would hide this fact of neurosis, Bukowski embraced it as real. He never doubted that he knew what others had on their minds and how all of the individuals he comes into glancing contact with had anything better to do with their time than to think about him and his current endeavor.

As is the case with virtually all Bukowski storylines, the promised fortune, in this case at the track, did not work out and Bukowski was left with nothing: no money and no women, returning to the mundane lifestyle of a postal worker. He states,

> *Somehow the money slipped away after that*
> *and soon I left the track and sat around my*
> *apartment waiting for the 90 days' leave to*
> *run out. My nerves were raw from the*
> *drinking and the action. It's not a new story*
> *about how women descends upon a man.*

To study the basis for this type of continued outcome in the writings of Bukowski, we come to understand that due to his continued early life failures, he embraced and came to be guided by the thought and ultimate result of failure. Bukowski, through life experience, continued to experience this, no doubt brought about by the excesses he attached to his life: alcoholism, gambling, paranoia, the craving to be a writer, and the lust after women. Therefore, these excesses, which often lead to failure, were bound to be translated into the lines of his literature.

Bukowski also details his sexual inadequacies, due to drink, in *Post Office*. He writes,

> *In bed I had something in front of me but I couldn't do anything with it. I whaled and I whaled and I whaled. Vi was very patient. I kept striving and banging but I had too much to drink. "Sorry baby," I rolled off and went to sleep.*

The ultimate inability to "Perform" haunted Bukowski throughout his life. He continually placed himself in positions where he would become drunk and, thus, would not have to ultimately take responsibilities for his actions, as was illustrated in the previous passage.

The brutal honesty in which Bukowski details his own inadequacies, alcohol induced or not, is highly expressive of his own mental state of mind and subconscious motivations. Whereas most authors would avoid statements such as the above, as it may be deemed to reflect upon their masculinity, Bukowski, on the other hand, placed the occurrence in his first novel.

The early failures of Bukowski's life and his being looked down upon by society never truly left Bukowski. From this, he gained the haunting ideology that he believed he was, in fact, a failure, prone to a constant state of loss. This fact is obvious in his approach to literature.

The mindset of failure followed Bukowski throughout his life, even when he had reached a certain plateau of success in his literary career and had purchased a house in San Pedro, California. This house had a mortgage of only $400.00 a month. Yet, Bukowski was constantly concerned if he would possess the monetary funds to pay the monthly payments on the home.

Factotum, published in 1975 by Black Sparrow Press, is a novel written in Bukowski fashion, made up of numerous short stories. As was the case with *Post Office, Factotum* can only be loosely viewed as a novel, in the traditional sense, as its short stories, though following a relatively linear path, often times have little to do with one another when viewing the novel as a whole. Cherkovski states,

> *He had come up with the title one day while thumbing through the dictionary: he happened across the word and, seeing the definition, decided that it fit him back in his forties, the period discussed: "a jack of all trade..." The title came easily, but the writing hadn't: he worked on the book sporadically through late 1973 and into the following year. In the fall of 1974 he put the book on the back burner, but he finished it in time for publication in 1975.*

116

Factotum sees, Henry Chinaski, the alter ego of Bukowski, arrived in New Orleans with his cardboard suitcase at 5:00 AM on a rainy morning.

> *Well, it was a new town. Maybe I'd get lucky. The rain stopped and the sun came out. I was in the black district. I walked along slowly. "Hey, poor white trash!" I put my suitcase down. A high yellow was sitting on the porch steps swinging her legs. She did look good. "Hello, poor white trash!" I didn't say anything. I just stood stood there looking at her. "How'd you like a piece of my ass, poor white trash?" She laughed at me. She had her legs crossed high and she kicked her feet; she had nice legs, high heels, and she kicked her legs and laughed. I picked up my suitcase and began to approach her up the walk. As I did I noticed a side curtain on a window to my left move just a bit. I saw a black man's face. He looked like Jersey Joe Wolcot. I backed down the pathway to the sidewalk. Her laughter followed me down the street.*

In the opening pages of this novel, we see that Bukowski was again reliving a trip he made to New Orleans, a journey often referenced in his poetry and short stories. The critical details of this story are presented in a more concrete fashion than in his previous novel *Post Office*. We see that what transpired over the period of four years between these two novels is that his thoughts became more consciously invoked; they were well thought out as opposed to simply being drunken ramblings.

Progression, in terms of the published novels and short story collections of Bukowski during the 1960's, and 1970's, was never represented by a dramatic change of style, as is the case with many authors, where you can clearly define an early, middle, and mature level of their individual literary styling. In the case of Bukowski, in no small part due to the age he was when he broke onto the literary scene, his mindset and writing style were already well matured. The noticeable changes which took place in his short story and novel writing techniques, throughout the main part of his literary career, are minimal, at best, noticeable only to the conscious reader who studies his work as a whole.

In the case of *Factotum* many of the stories told are ones that had appeared in various other forms of poetry or prose in other books. Therefore, no new ground was broken with the publication of this novel—it was simply another vehicle for the Bukowski myth to be propagated.

Bukowski, in this novel, relives the temporary nature of all of his employment and relationships. As is the case with all of his novels, he rarely pays a passing notice to the fact that a job or a relationship is over. He is more prone to attach a jealous note to the fact that his previous mate may have a new lover than to even look deeply into his emotions and express any true sense of loss at their being gone.

As is illustrated in the proceeding passage, Bukowski continually turns to alcohol as a means to deal with any emotions of loss and enters into a drunken period to over come the sense of alienation he may possess. Again, we can trace these glassed over emotions to his childhood, when he developed a strong defense mechanism to deal with the shame he felt brought on by his heritage and his family's behavior.

> *I got my first paycheck and moved out of Jan's place and into an apartment of my own. When I came home one night, she had moved in with me. What the fuck, I told her, my land is your land. Shortly thereafter, we had our worst fight. She left and I got drunk for three days and three nights. When I sobered up I knew my job was gone. I never went back. I decided to clean up the apartment. I vacuumed the floors, scrubbed the window ledges, scoured the bathtub and sink, waxed the kitchen floor, killed all the spiders and roaches, emptied and washed the ashtrays, washed the dishes, scrubbed the kitchen sink, hung up clean towels and installed a new roll of toilet paper. I must be turning into a fag, I thought.*

During the early to mid 1970's, Bukowski lived the life of a wandering drunken poet, being flown from poetry reading to poetry reading around the United States. This was the "Golden Age" for Bukowski as he was allowed to travel, as he had done as a wandering young man. The difference during this period of time, however, was he was the center of attention, thus, his long years of alienation and numerous poems and short stories written about the subject were met with new found cheers of acceptance.

Poetry was obviously the heart of Bukowski's literary skills and his desired form of expression. Poetry could be instantaneously written and it did not take the amount of time and rewrites which the composing of a novel demanded. In a conversation with Neeli Cherkovski, Bukowski states,

> *Martin just waits for the poems and then he puts them in a book form. All I have to do is let the typewriter write them down for me. Then, of course, I have to send them off. It's a hard life, kid.*

Between *Factotum* and *Women,* Bukowski published a collection of poems, written during this period of his life, entitled, *Love is a Dog From Hell: Poems 1974—1977.* He writes in the poem,

> *quite clean girls in gingham dresses,*
> *all I've ever known are whores,*
> *ex prostitutes,*
> *madwomen. I see men with quiet,*
> *gentle women—I see them in the supermarkets,*
> *I see them walking down the streets together,*
> *I see them in their apartments: people at peace, living together. I know that their peace is only partial, but there is peace, often hours and days of peace.*
> *all I've ever known are pill freaks, alcoholics,*
> *whores, ex-prostitutes, madwomen.*
> *when one leaves*
> *another arrives*
> *worse than her predecessor.*

From the above writing it can be seen that the Bukowski myth is continued by the author. At this period of time, the mid 1970's, Bukowski poetry has still not yet become well known. His works are predominately read among a small group of counter culture people who explore the avant-garde literary realms. Thus, Bukowski felt the need to continue to publicize himself in his writings.

The poetry that makes up this book is the first collection where it can be seen, when viewed by chronological content that Bukowski has locked deeply into a style and a theme for his subject matter. From this point forward, in his poetry, he reveals no new levels of exploration. Instead, from this point forward, he will continually return to similar storylines, told in similar fashion throughout the remainder of his life.

Gerald Locklin, in his essay, *Bukowski's War All the Time* and *Horses Don't Bet On People & Neither Do I*, comments,

> *Readers are still surprised to find Bukowski employing the same stories in poems, Short stories, and novels. They seem to feel there is a law against this, maybe such a prohibition is taught in some creative writing class, but I have yet to see it written down.*

From a singular perspective, the fact that Bukowski continued to return to the same subject matter can be viewed from the understanding that he had simply defined what worked for him, in terms of literature, and he, therefore, continues to revisit the subject matter. From a deeper perspective, however, one can see that the aging

Bukowski had reached a point in his life where his definition of himself, how he was perceived by the reading public, and what method works to perpetuate the Bukowski myth had become so ingrained in his mind that he no longer chose to explore new avenues of expression.

What becomes obvious when one studies the poetry of Bukowski is that he wanted to maintain the ongoing probability of new publications of his work. To this end, he composed poetry of a strikingly similar content. From the publication of this collection of poetry onward, it can be understood that Bukowski's poetry is Bukowski's poetry—whether it was composed in the late 1960's or the late 1980's, its motif was constant.

Women was published by Black Sparrow Press in 1978. Bukowski's character, in this novel, took on the pseudonym he commonly used in his writings, Henry Chinaski. The book opens with the passage,

> *I was 50 years old and hadn't been to bed with a women for four years. I had no women friends. I looked at them as I passed them on the streets or wherever I saw them, but I looked at them without yearning and with a sense of futility. I masturbated regularly, but the idea of having a relationship with a woman—even on non-sexual terms—was beyond my imagination.*

We see that in these well-chosen words, Bukowski autobiographically details the torments of an aging man. Though he is well respected, among the counter culture, by this point in his literary career, the ravages of his early psychological conditioning, continued alcoholism, and the simple fact of aging have taken him to a point in his life where he no longer feels that interactions with women are possible.

As previously detailed, early in Bukowski's literary career he became labeled as a hater of women by critics due to the literary content he used in depicting his interrelationship with the female gender. Though many critics would argue that this fact never truly changed with Bukowski and his writings, Dr. Russell Harrison believes,

> *By the time Bukowski came to write Women, however, this had begun to change and his depiction of Women and sexual relationships gradually shifted from crude descriptions of events and flat characterizations of women to fuller descriptions, more rounder character-izations and female characters who, it was suggested had lived lives outside the orbit of Henry Chinaski.*

When one studies the content and the structure of the stories which make up *Women*, it can be concluded that Bukowski's attitude towards the literary description of women was, in fact, no doubt changing by this period in his life, even if the graphic descriptions of his sexual antics were not. The factors that brought about this change were twofold. First of all, Bukowski had become older. At the time this novel was published, he was fifty-five years old. His emotional temperament had, no doubt, mellowed by this stage of his life. The second factor has to do with the notoriety he had achieved by this point in his literary career. With this fame, came the influx of more substantial and educated females. Therefore, he came to be surrounded by a more refined group of people, ultimately changing his attitude towards women on the whole.

When one studies the writings which make up, *Women,* one can witness that Bukowski never so much hated or despised females, but was, in fact, desirous of long term acceptance from them. He desired intimacy, yet, as he had often times been rejected, as a younger man, he hid behind alcoholism and temporal meaningless relationships to protect himself from the pain of what he believed would ultimately occur, namely, rejection.

To illustrate this point we can view a relationship that Bukowski details in *Women.*

> *We kissed in the dark. I was a kiss freak anyway, and Sara was one of the best kissers I had ever met. I'd have to go all the way back to Lydia to find anyone comparable. Yet each woman was different, each kissed in her own way. Lydia was probably kissing some son of a bitch right now, or worse, kissing his parts.*

Bukowski's affection for this woman was obvious. Yet, in the middle of enjoying a session of kissing, with a woman he not only found attractive but also described to be a great kisser, he could not remove his mind from the relationships that had gone before. Thus, he not only predicted this relationship to end in a similar fashion but set the destructive life factors he embraced into motion which would bring about this ultimate demise.

As stated at the beginning of this study, Bukowski's life could not be separated from his literature. In the case above, it is almost irrelevant whether or not this situation actually occurred, because from it, we see how the mind of Bukowski worked. No matter what he was experiencing in the moment, he could not remove the memories of pain and rejection from the past.

For Bukowski it was much easier to go into the graphic description of a sexual encounter than to evaluate the deeply rooted realities of his relationships and his own psyche. He writes,

> *Sara had my cock in her hand, petting it, rubbing it. Then she pressed it against her cunt. She rubbed it up and down, up and down against her cunt. She was obeying her God, Drayer Baba. I didn't play with her cunt because I felt that would offend Drayer. We kissed and she kept rubbing my cock against her cunt, or maybe against her clit, I didn't know. I waited for her to put my cock in her cunt. But she kept rubbing. The hairs began to burn my cock. I pulled away.*

Bukowski's autobiographical musings were often punctuated by his description of the mean-streets of the world where he found himself dwelling. With this he could quickly shift attention away from the more profound issues of self and relationships, which he never truly dealt with, and move the focus of the storyline onto the urban world which, through his style of story telling, one can conclude that he believed he had no ultimate control over. As was often the case with

Bukowski's writings, he would go into descriptions of his Hollywood lifestyle. He did this in *Women.*

> *I felt peaceful in Playa del Rey. It was good to get out of the crowded, dirty court where I lived. There was no shade, and the sun beat down mercilessly on us. We were all insane in one way or another. Even the dogs and the cats were insane, and the birds and the newboys and the hookers. For us, in east Hollywood, the toilets never worked properly and the landlord's cut-rate plumbers could never quite fix them. We left the tank lids off and hand-manipulated the plunger. The faucets dripped, the roaches crawled, the dogs crapped everywhere, and the screens had large Holes in them that let in flies and all manner of strange flying insect.*

The graphic description of the court apartments Bukowski lived in on Carlton Way and De Longpre Avenue in Hollywood not only draws a very accurate picture of the setting of this location and the occurrences which took place there, but writing of his dwellings in the style which he did also allows the reader to again be drawn into the Bukowski myth of the down and out artist living on the fringes of society. Bukowski, who had seen and experienced the better living conditions of many of his friends, could detail this locale from the perspective of someone from the outside looking in. As many of the ethnically diverse people who lived in this area, at the time Bukowski was a resident in the 1960's and 1970's, had come from much worse living conditions and thus believed they were living well, Bukowski on the other hand detailed the seedy side of this neighborhood, writing for the eye of his readers.

Bukowski continually describes his dwellings in the most inhospitable manner possible. From a literary standpoint this can be viewed as a descriptive artistic statement. However, when we look deeper into Bukowski the man, we see that due to his own psychological insecurities he bound himself to the lifestyle of the lower classes, for here he would not be negatively judged, as could occur if he chose to move upward to the more appealing sections of the city.

Ham on Rye, published in 1982, is Bukowski's memoir of his early years. This novel is virtually an autobiography broken up into short stories and memories of his life. This collection is written in the very straightforward fashion, which Bukowski came to embrace. Neeli Cherkovski details,

> *When Hank began writing Ham on Rye in 1980, he opened up memories that had long lain dormant. The book is a song for L.A., crowded with images of the city in the twenties and the life among lower-middle-class Angelinos during the great depression. When the echoes of Andernach, which begin the book, turn into graphic descriptions of beatings by an angry father, the mythic Bukowski/Chinaski emerges.*

Bukowski was sixty years old when he began this novel. He had reached a point in his life where he was entirely supported by his writings, he had been in an on-again off-again relationship with the same woman, Linda King, for several years and he was left living the role of the character he had created in his poetry, short stories, and novels. With this book, Bukowski was able to focus on much of the pain of his childhood and if not come to terms with it, at least feel the freedom of the baring of his soul for the whole world to see.

Russell Harrison in his essay, *Politics, Class, and the Plebeian Tradition*, states,

> *For several reasons Ham on Rye is the most satisfying of Bukowski's novels. First of all, it is here he treats in a serious and extended Fashion a number of the issues that remained unexamined in his earlier novels: relations with and between his parents, relations to the social world of his peers.*
> *Bukowski begins the novel,*
> *The first thing I remember is being under something. It was a table, I saw a table leg, I saw the legs of the people, and the portion of the tablecloth hanging down. It was dark under there, I like being under there.*

This novel was, of course, written from the mind of an aging man who had spent the better part of his existence being a proud drunkard. In addition, the identification with the character he created for himself, in his written words, was so prominent in his mind; it is hard to believe that Bukowski himself could have separated himself from it. As we see in this opening passage of this book, Bukowski wanted to portray this lonely, sullen individual even in this novel. Thus, we can clearly see that though the memories that make up the stories that fill this book are, no doubt, based in fact, they too are clouded with the Bukowski myth.

> *Jr. high went by quick enough. About 8th grade, going into the 9th, I broke out with acne. Many of the guys had it but not like mine. Mine was really terrible. I was the worst case in town. I had pimples and boils all over my face, back, neck, and some on my chest. It happened just as I was beginning to be accepted as a tough guy and a leader. I was still tough but it wasn't the same. I had to withdraw. I watched people from afar, it was like a stage play. Only they were the stage   and   I   was   the audience of one.*

With this statement, we see that in Bukowski's memory his true separation from society and his advancement to functional adulthood was hampered by something completely out of his control, a medical condition; acne. From here, the world became a stage to Bukowski, a place where he could watch the action but never truly be a part of. This acne condition, in association with his dysfunctional family life, lead him into his alcoholism which ultimately provided a point of focus and a basis for him to achieve greatness as a bohemian author.

Black Sparrow Press published *Hot Water Music,* in 1984. It is a collection of thirty-six short stories. In a conversation with Neeli Cherkovski, Bukowski describes the book. He states,

> *These stories are different than the earlier ones. They're cleaner, closer to the vest. I'm*

trying for clarity. I think I've really done it here.

Bukowski, who had always been a vocal critic of authors he did and did not like, finds himself critiquing his own newly created collection of short stories. From this statement it is revealed that he was not the anarchist writer that many critics believed him to be. In fact, at least by this stage of his career, he took the application of what he did very seriously.

Hot Water Music focuses upon the exceedingly graphic style of Bukowski literature. In this collection, Bukowski embraced shock value, seemingly for its effect alone. Additionally, in terms of style, *Hot Water Music* finds Bukowski shifting between first-person and narrative story telling. This was not entirely new to him, as a small number of his short stories and a larger number of his poems previously found him reaching into this level of literature.

Bukowski was never a master of third-person literature. When he delved into this style of writing, it was more an exercise in his telling a very concise story from a very Bukowskian point of view, rather than the work of a master novelist. Bukowski writes,

> *Meg and Tony got his wife to the airport. After Dolly was airborne they stopped in the airport bar for a drink. Meg had a whiskey and soda. Tony had a scotch and water.*
> *"Your wife trust you," said Meg.*
> *"Yeh," said Tony.*
> *"I wonder if I can trust you?"*

"Don't you like to be fucked?"
"That's not the point."
"What's the point?"
"The point is that Dolly and I are friends."
"We can be friends."
"Not that way."
"Be modern. It's the modern age. People swing. They're uninhibited. They fuck from the ceiling. They screw dogs, babies, chickens, fish..."
"I like to choose. I have to care."

In terms of literary grace, this opening section of Bukowski's short story, *Strokes to Nowhere,* cannot be viewed as exceptionally eloquent in formation or style. When viewed as an expression of simple literary depiction, however, we can see it as an example of the Bukowski style of literature, where the need for absolute description is not necessary and the Zen like freedom of simply telling the story is embraced.

In the story, *I Love You Albert,* Bukowski again writes the story in the form of a narrative.

They got into the elevator and Myra began pressing the buttons. The elevator went up, it went down, it stopped, and Myra kept asking, "Where do you live?" And Louie kept repeating, "Fourth floor, apartment number four." Myra kept pushing the buttons while the elevator went up and down. "Listen," she finally said, "we've been on this thing for years. I'm sorry but I've got to piss." "O.K.," said Louie, "let's make a deal. You let me work the buttons and I'll let you piss." "Done," she said, and she pulled her panties down, squatted and did the deed. As he watched it trickle across the floor Louie punched the "4" button. They arrived. By then Myra had straightened, pulled up herpanties, and was ready to exit.

The stories told in this collection appear to be much more contrived to invoke an emotional response than to truly tell a story worth depicting. Bukowski himself, however, believed *Hot Water Music,* was a well-written book.

Hot Water Music is important, according to Hank, because it represents a newer, freer style of writing,

explains Neeli Cherkovski.

When the text of *Hot Water Music* is studied, however, it is entirely the opposite of the free form literature Bukowski came to be identified as creating. The fact that Bukowski saw this book as something that it was not, allows us to peer into the mindset of the author at this time of his life, when he was sixty-four years old. By this point in his literary career, Bukowski had lived the gambit of the down and out writer, the marginally accepted author, and the highly sought after reader on the poetry circuit. What he was perceiving about his writing, at this age and at this point of his career, was no longer a profound and unhindered vision. What he saw, instead, was clouded not only by his years of alcoholism, but by his own continuing publicizing of himself and how he desired the critical literary media to perceive the work he created.

Bukowski, by this point in his literary career, was no longer an organic product of his own device. He was instead, a writer creating what was expected of him: shock literature. This is, no doubt, the reason that critics who were once appalled by his brazen approach to writing were not finally putting his work into the context of Bukowskian literature and analyzing it as the style of literature created by a continually active, single pointed, writer, instead of simply discarding it as, "Blatant Misogynism." The problem this apparent acceptance caused Bukowski was that it locked him into a prescribed literary format. Thus, he could not allow his current experiences in life to be deeply involved in his work, as he believed, who would want to read about what a senior citizen had for lunch, all-be-it, a hard drinking senior citizen

Russell Harrison in his essay, *The Fascination of the (Extra)ordinary: The Short Stories of Charles Bukowski* writes of how Bukowski's approach to sexuality in this collection of short stories has changed. He states,

> *The subtle changes in context and the ironic humor of the sexual descriptions preclude any suggestion of the formulaic. The "banality" of the events described does not differ that much from the subject of the earlier stories, but they are no longer "naive" and "spontaneous" in their presentation.*

Through Bukowski's long years of composing literature, he had gone through numerous experiences—aging being, no doubt, the most influential. By this point in his literary career, with his age advancing and his literary style defined, Bukowski's literature had become a byproduct of his own myth.

Bukowski composed three very short novels after *Hot Water Music;* they were: *Bring Me Your Love,* (1983), *There's No Business,* (1984), both illustrated by the artist R. Crumb, and *The Day it Snowed in L.A.* (1986) Each of these three novels are written in the third-person and are made up of no more than fifteen pages of actual text. In fact, *The Day it Snowed in L.A.* is composed in the fashion of a comic strip, complete with childlike drawings. The texts for, *Bring Me Your Love* and *There's No Business,* minus the R. Crumb illustration, were additionally published in the 1990 Black Sparrow Press collection of recent Bukowski short stories and poems, *Septuagenarian Stew.*

These three works were not revolutionary in the content or style. They saw publication solely because of the fact that Bukowski, by this point in his career, had the ability to tap into a certain percentage of the literary reading public who would be attracted to this type of short-run publication.

The structure and content of these books can be seen in, *Bring Me Your Love,* where Bukowski writes,

> *"Well," she asked, "how's the little wifrey?"*
> *Harry poured a drink and sat down beside her.*
> *"I'm sorry, Nan. . . ."*
> *"Sorry for what, for who? For her or for me?"*
> *Harry drained his shot of whiskey.*

*"Let's not make a goddamned soap opera
out of this thing.'
"Oh yeah? Well, what do you want to make
out of it? A simple roll in the hay? You want
to try to finish? Or would you rather go in
the bathroom and beat off?"*

It can be understood that had Bukowski
begun his publishing career with third-person
novellas such as this, one could view them as
elementary works that lead, latter, to a more
profound vision of literature. On the other hand,
when one views these three books as being written
late into Bukowski's career, they can be understood
to be solely the literature created by a man who had
written and rewritten all he had to say about the
continually relived subjects of life he had time and
time again detailed.

Bukowski had, by the point of the
composition of these three works, been involved
with and eventually married to Linda King for a
long period of time. With this, came a monogamous
relationship, and though he continued to drink and
visit the race track, his inspiration for new views on
love affairs and the interactive stimuli gained from
said, were removed from his life. Bukowski, due to
his age and his marriage, had no new erotic
inspiration. Thus, he fell into the habit of
composing literature from the basis of memory and
in the style of accepted literary structure. Though
no new literary ground was broken with these three
short novels, the observation of this fact does, none-
the-less, lead one to understand more clearly the
evolution of Bukowski, the literary artist.

The continued return to known Bukowski
territory can be can be observed in his poetry, as

well. In his 1986 collection of poems, *You Get So Alone At Times That It Just Makes Sense,* he writes,

I can remember starving in a
small room in a strange city
shades pulled down, listening to
classical music
I was young I was so young it hurt like a
knife inside
because there was no alternative except to
hide as long as possible -
not in self-pity but with dismay at my limited
chance:
trying to connect.

Almost as a cry for understanding for the unresolved pain of youth, Bukowski, a man now in his sixties, cries out in this poem. In this work, he addresses the grief he still possesses decades later for himself, as a young man, on the road. He never refers to the fact that his own alcoholism helped to generate his alienation which came to define his life, nor does he mention the fact that he spent two years at Los Angeles City College before taking off and seeking publishing success in distant cities. As is the case with many aging people, no matter how successful they ultimately become, they come to look back on their life with certain remaining pain and regrets. In the case of Bukowski, his vehicle for the dissemination of these emotions was his poetry.

Within this previous poetic passage, even though emotional distress is pervasive, Bukowski continues to depict the youthful rebel who, while struggling against the world, possesses a fondness for the arts—in this case, classical music. This theme of a love for classical music and opera is a

136

constant throughout the literature of Bukowski. As if making a subliminal statement intended to lead the reading masses to the musical art form, he continually refers to his listening to classical music.

As seen in this poem, decades before its composition, Bukowski wrote that he believed he had little chance of connection or becoming socially normal, yet, that is, in fact, exactly what came of his life. He was married, had friends, and if any remaining social alienation was present, it was self-inflicted.

Septuagenarian Stew, published in 1990, is a combination of ninety-eight short stories and poems. This was the first collection of Bukowski's work that was published in this consolidated fashion.

The short stories that make up *Septuagenarian Stew* are composed in a combination of first and third-person stylings. These stories continually reference a younger Bukowski. In the story, *No Love Songs,* he writes,

> *Dear Editor:*
> *I realize I missed the deadline but I've been beset by trivialities, like arguments with the female, car breakdowns, a houseguest for one week, and various other things I can't remember. One I can remember is that I had to get my driver's license renewed. Each time I get my driver's license renewed I begin to realize how much older I am, it's a sign that you're moving along toward the grave, a more telling sign than New Year's Eve or birthdays, and although I really don't mind dying I do dislike the certainty of it. So every four years at driver's license renewal*

time I decided to go on one   huge   drunk.
So, having done that, I was driving along the
next day, towards the Hollywood Dept. of
Motor Vehicles but my head hurt too much
to face it. And I kept blacking out. So I took
a right, found a bar up near Hollywood
Boulevard, I   think I was on Las Palmas or
Cherokee, parked, got out, went in, sat
down, got a Heineken from the barkeep, no
glass, and took a good long haul.

In this story, the reader again witnesses
Bukowski writing about occurrences that took place
years before. At the time of composing this story
Bukowski was in his late sixties. We see that this
aging process was paramount in his mind. He did
not regard this natural process as transformation in
the realms of human growth and advancing
understanding, as did Marguerite Duras. Instead, it
was a mournful time, when the only antidote was to
get drunk; as drinking was the only remedy
Bukowski knew.

The poetry that makes up *Septuagenarian
Stew* is typically Bukowskian. He writes in, *the
girls and the birds,*

> *the girls were young*
> *and worked the*
> *streets*
> *but often couldn't*
> *score, they*
> *ended up*
> *in my hotel*
> *room*
> *3 or 4 of*
> *them*

sucking at the
wine,
hair in face,
runs in
stockings,
cursing, telling
stories.

As financial success came upon Bukowski, he would occasionally mention this fact in his short stories and poems. This was the case of one poem presented in this collection, entitled, gold in your eye. He writes,

I got into my BMW and drove to my bank to
pick up my American Express Gold Card.
I told the girl at the desk what I wanted.
"you're Mr. Chinaski," she said.
"yes, you want some i.d.?"
"oh no, we know you..."
I slipped the card into my wallet
went back to the parking
got into the BMW (paid for, straight cash)
and decided to drive down to the liquor
store.

From this poem, it is obvious that Bukowski wished to portray his success and his notoriety, in addition to remaining tied to his fame-making alcoholism. Bukowski, having spent much of his life interacting with the lower levels of society, certainly deserved to indulge himself with the occasionally boastful poem.

The references to his wealth and to the racetrack are the only two current experiences that Bukowski would allude to in his poetry, at this late period of his life. Though Bukowski often referred to himself as an old man in his writings, it is unfortunate that he did not describe his reaction to the process of aging more precisely. For from this, the Bukowski reader would have been led deeper into his frame of mental reference. But, as described in the previous poem, Bukowski did not view aging as a positive experience. Thus, he obviously did not wish to conquer the subject in his writings.

Pulp, was Bukowski's last novel published while he was still alive. It was completed just before his death in 1994. It is written in the Mickey Spillane styling. It is the tale of a down and out private detective sent on a hunt by a beautiful woman. The novel opens,

> *I was sitting in my office, my lease had expired and McKelvey was starting eviction proceedings. It was a hellish hot day and the air conditioner was broken. A fly crawled across the top of my desk. I reached out with the open palm of my hand and sent him out of the game. I wiped my hand on my right pant leg as the phone rang. I picked it up, "Ah yes," I said. "Do you read Celine?" a female voice asked. Her voice sounded quite sexy. I had been lonely for some time. Decades.*

As this novel was different from all other Bukowski works, the question can be posed, was this novel a new expression of Bukowskian literature? The answer would be, no.

In this novel, Bukowski presents subject matter and style completely taken from another author. Spillane is an author whom he never criticized or complimented in any of his early works, something that he commonly did to all authors that he thought worthy of his attention either in a positive or negative sense. Therefore, it can be surmised that Bukowski, at this point of his life, when he had become ill from leukemia, wrote this novel simply to have an activity that he could focus his attention upon. This novel is obviously a parody of another famed author's style of literature. Thus, no new literary ground was uncovered by Bukowski with its composition and no new literary revolutions started.

As Bukowski aged, his provocative literature appeared to wane. This can be seen in his approach to the subject of eroticism in this novel, which he written about more in jest, than in the actual acutely descriptive passages he had become known for. He writes of a conversation with a telephone sex solicitor,

> *"Well, you sound like you have a cold. Maybe you smoke too many cigarettes."*
> *"I only smoke one thing, Nick!"*
> *"What's that, Kitty?"*
> *"Can't you guess?"*
> *"Nah..."*
> *"Look down at yourself, Nick."*
> *"O.k."*
> *"What do you see?"*
> *"Drink, telephone..."*
> *"What else, Nicky?"*
> *"My shoes..."*
> *"Nick, what's that big thing sticking out there as you talk to me?"*
> *"Oh, that! That's my gut!"*

The subdued nature of the subject matter Bukowski covered in his last five novels, including the three novellas previously discussed, was the reason the critics began to take a less harsh view of the author. It was not that Bukowski had necessarily changed his drunken attitudes, it was simply the fact that he had become old and had settled into the lifestyle of a married man, who found his joy in frequenting the race track, drinking alone, and sitting by his small pool in the backyard of his San Pedro, California home.

By his sixties, the critics no longer attacked the writings of Bukowski, they were much more interested in the acting performance of Ben Gazzara in the first film based on Bukowski's life, *Tales of Ordinary Madness,* or the directing approach of the Belgian film maker, Dominique Deruddere, in his idealized depiction of Bukowski in, *Love is a Dog from Hell,* or in the fact that Mickey Rourke won out over Sean Penn for the lead acting role in the Bukowski composed film, *Barfly.* The literary critics, from Bukowski's early career forward, have continually looked beyond the true Bukowski, only witnessing the superficial level of his creations and not his contributions to the literary world as a whole. From this standpoint of prejudice, the reading public was never led to the works of Bukowski, as was done for so many less deserving authors. In addition, Bukowski, as an author, has continued to be overlooked by the literary world. His name is not mentioned in the majority of the reference journals that list American authors. It is only now, after his death that studies have begun to be published on his work and the true literary contributions of Bukowski are beginning to be recognized.

As we have seen, Bukowski could never leave the negative experiences of his childhood and young adult life behind. Instead, by his embellishing them, he used the thoughts and ideologies of an admitted neurotic and expanded the literary art form to a new and unexplored level. As Steve Richmond writes,

> *I asked Hank for advice—once he said, "DRINK, WRITE, AND FUCK."*

This statement ideally depicts the life philosophy of Charles Bukowski.

Bukowski died of Leukemia in San Pedro, California on March 9, 1994 at the age of seventy-three. He had relocated to this sleepy harbor community a decade before in order to gain needed separation from his friends and limited adoring fans who kept him drunk and distracted from his necessary writing. In San Pedro, he found needed seclusion while still remaining in close proximity to old, seedy naval bars and his beloved racetrack.

Death was never far from Bukowski, though he beat the Grim Reaper for longer than could have been expected from a *man who lived the lifestyle he chose. As he wrote in, Notes of a Dirty Old Man,*

> *he sometimes even thought of taking his own life. a few years earlier I awakened from a week's drunk and pretty determined to kill myself. I was shacked with a sweet little thing at the time and not working. the money was gone, the rent was due, and even if I had been able to find a flunk's job of some sort, that would have only seemed like another kind of death. I decided to kill*

myself when she left the room the first time. mean while, I went outside on the streets, slightly curious, just slightly, as to what the day it was. on our drunks, days and nights ran together. we just drank and made love continually. it was about noon and I walked down the hill to check the corner newspaper for the day. Friday the paper said. well, Friday seemed as good a day as any. then I saw the headline. MILTON BERLE'S COUSIN HIT ON THE HEAD BY FALLING ROCKS. now how the hell are you going to kill yourself when they write headlines like that?

From chance situations like these, Bukowski continued to live and eventually write his perceptions and experiences for the eyes of the world. From this, was born a new era in modern erotic bohemian literature, paying homage to the drink, the track, the girls, the sex, and the nonstop disassociation from the accepted realms of reality.

Conclusion

The literary critics embraced marguerite Duras; Charles Bukowski was shunned. Duras' adult life was spent predominately living in comfort, while Bukowski's was spent, at least until his fifties, embraced by the downtrodden on the hard edge of society. Duras depicted the erotic as endeavors against the norm of society; Bukowski took the subject of erotica to its most animalistic level. From the literature these two authors created, one is allowed a poignant view of both the female and male perception of eroticism. Though their writings differed in content and context, they both were uniquely revealing in their own approach to modern erotic literature.

From viewing the lives and the literary works of Marguerite Duras and Charles Bukowski we can come to understand that they were both individuals who, due to their exposure to dysfunctional family situations came to make life altering choices, at a young age, born out of emotional instabilities: Duras had an affair with an older Asian man, Bukowski embraced alcohol. Both of these authors seeking the acceptance that they did not find at home or in their surrounding society, embraced their chosen intoxicant, which was to prove would shape and dominate the rest of their individual lives. Whereas most individuals who live a life defined by indulgence find themselves engulfed by the expanding negative addiction of the experience, Duras and Bukowski, maintaining the psychological alienation which was present in their childhood, and, thus, continuing to seek further external acceptance, wrote down their life experiences for the world to read. From this highly therapeutic action, they ultimately created not only moving but revolutionary twentieth century erotic literature.

Works Cited

Ames, Sanford Scribner, Ed., Remains to Be Seen: Essays on Marguerite Duras. New York: Peter Lang, 1988.p.107, p. 172

Bukowski, Charles, Bring Me Your Love. Santa Barbara: Black Sparrow Press, 1983. p. 14

--, Burning In Water Drowning in Flame. Santa Barbara: Black Sparrow Press, 1983. p. 132

--, Factotum. Santa Barbara: Black Sparrow Press: 1982. pp. 11-12, pp. 139-140

--, Ham on Rye. Santa Barbara: Black Sparrow Press, 1983.p. 9

--, Hot Water Music. Santa Barbara: Black Sparrow Press, 1984. p. 67, pp. 131-132

--, Love is a Dog From Hell. Santa Barbara: Black Sparrow Press, 1983. p. 74

--, Mocking Bird Wish Me Luck. Santa Barbara: Black Sparrow Press, 1982. p. 46, p.188

--, Notes of a Dirty Old Man. San Francisco: City Lights Books, 1969. p. 11, p. 12, pp. 12-13, p. 77, p. 118, p. 238

--, Post Office. Santa Barbara: Black Sparrow Press, 1984.p. 9, p. 33, p. 72, p. 81, p. 84

--, Pulp. Santa Barbara: Black Sparrow Press, 1996. p. 9, p. 172

--, Septuagenarian Stew. Santa Rose: Black Sparrow Press 1996. p. 70, p. 258, p. 298

--, South of No North. Santa Barbara: Black Sparrow Press, 1984. p. 93, p. 105, p. 125

--, Tales of Ordinary Madness. San Francisco: City Lights Books, 1983. p. 82, p. 127, p. 145, p. 160

--, The Days Run Away Like the Wild Horses Over the Hills. Santa Barbara: Black Sparrow Press, 1983. p. 130

--, The Most Beautiful Woman in Town and Other Stories. San Francisco: City Lights Books, 1983. p. 61

--, Women. Santa Barbara: Black Sparrow Press, 1983. p. 7, p. 212, p. 224

--, You Get So Alone At Times That It Just Makes Sense. Santa Barbara: Black Sparrow Press, 1986. p. 139

Cherkovski, Neeli, Ferlinghetti: A Biography. New York: Doubleday, 1977. pp. 195-196

--, Hank: The Life of Charles Bukowski. New York: Random House, 1991. p. 5, p. 11, p. 35, p. 118, p. 160, p. 186, p. 243, p. 245, p. 274, p. 276, p. 300, p. 302

Cismaru, Alfred, Marguerite Duras, New York: Twayne Publishers, 1971. p.108

Cooney, Seamus, ed. Charles Bukowski: Living On Luck: Select Letters 1960s-1970s. Santa Rosa: Black Sparrow Press, 1995. p. 68, p. 106, p. 146

--, Charles Bukowski: Screams from the Balcony: Select Letters 1960-1970. Santa Rosa: Black Sparrow Press, 1994. p. 104

Duras, Marguerite, Blue Eyes, Black Hair. New York: Pantheon Books, 1987. p. 1, p. 79

--, Destroy She Said. New York: Grove Weinenfield, 1970. p. 3 p. 19, p. 31, p. 44 p. 87

--, Duras by Duras. San Francisco: City Lights Books, 1987 p. 14, p. 15, p. 75, p. 92

--, The Lover. New York: Perennial Library, 1985. p. 3, p. 4,p. 12, p. 13, p. 16, pp. 17-18, p. 25, p. 37, pp. 42 – 43, p. 57, p. 89, pp. 116-117

--, The Malady of Death. New York: Grove Press, 1982. p. 1, p. 37, p. 50, p. 60

--, The North China Lover. New York: The New Press, 1992. p. 1, p. 2, p. 66, p. 69, p. 158.

--, Practicalities. New York: Grove Weidenfield, 1987. pp. 23-24, p. 38

--, The Ravishing of Lol Stein. New York: Pantheon Books, 1966. pp. 2 –3, p. 71, p. 125.

--, The Sea Wall. New York: Farrar, Straus, & Giroux, 1952. p. 54, p. 180. p.206, p.209

--, Two By Duras. Toronto: Coach House Press, 1982. p. 77

--, Yann Andrea Steiner. New York: Charles Scribner's Son, 1992. pp. 20-21, p. 58

Duras, Marguerite & Gauthier, Xaviere, Woman to Woman. Lincoln: University of Nebraska Press, 1987. p.1

Harrison, Russell, Against the American Dream: Essays on Charles Bukowski. Santa Rosa: Black Sparrow Press, 1995. pp. 18-19, p. 162, p. 183, p. 184, p. 255, p. 259

Locklin, Gerald, Charles Bukowski: A Sure Bet. Sudbury: Water Row Press, 1996. p. 3, p. 36

Richmond, Steve, Spinning Off Bukowski. Northville: Sun Dog Press, 1996. p. 57

Schuster, Marilyn R., Marguerite Duras Revisited. New York: Twayne Publishers, 1993. p.1, p. 112

Selous, Trista, The Other Woman: Feminism and Femininity in the Works of Marguerite Duras. New York: Yale University Press, 1988. p 151

Vircondelet, Alain, Duras: A Biography. Normal: Dalkey Archive Press, 1994. p. 5, p.6

Bibliography

Aiello, John, Charles Bukowski's Hollywood Babylon. The San Francisco Chronicle, 20 June 1989, Edition: Final.

Ames, Sanford Scribner, Ed., Remains to Be Seen: Essays on Marguerite Duras. New York, Peter Lang, 1988

Andler, Suzanna, Ever So Gently Into Turmoil. The London Times, 26 January 1995.

Barnes, Julian, Duras, Her Memories, The War. The Washington Post, 18 May 1986.

Berne, Suzanne, For Patient Duras - Lovers. The San Francisco Chronicle, 10 January 1988.

Birkerts, Sven. Duras' The War: A Memoir is a Story of Pain, A Diary of Venerability. The Chicago Tribune, 13 April 1986

Bremmer, Charles, Author's Biography Draws Ire from Left Bank Literati, The London Times, 5 April 1994.

Bukowski, Charles, Again. The Los Angeles Times, 2 June 1996.

--, Barfly. Santa Barbara, The Magnet Press, 1984.

--, Bring Me Your Love. Santa Barbara, Black Sparrow Press, 1983.

--, Burning In Water Drowning in Flame. Santa Barbara, Black Sparrow Press, 1983.

--, Dangling In The Tournefortia. Santa Barbara, Black Sparrow Press, 1981.

--, Factotum. Santa Barbara, Black Sparrow Press, 1982.

--, Ham on Rye. Santa Barbara, Black Sparrow Press, 1983.

--, Hot Water Music. Santa Barbara, Black Sparrow Press, 1984.

--, Love is a Dog From Hell. Santa Barbara, Black Sparrow Press, 1983.

--, Mocking Bird Wish Me Luck. Santa Barbara, Black Sparrow Press, 1982.

--, Notes of a Dirty Old Man. San Francisco, City Lights Books, 1969.

--, Play the Piano Drunk Like a Percussion Instrument Until the Fingers Begin to Bleed a Bit. Santa Barbara, Black Sparrow Press, 1982.

--, Post Office. Santa Barbara, Black Sparrow Press, 1984.

--, Pulp. Santa Barbara, Black Sparrow Press, 1996.

--, Septuagenarian Stew. Santa Rose, Black Sparrow Press 1996.

--, Shakespeare Never Did This. San Francisco, City Lights Books, 1979.

--, South of No North. Santa Barbara, Black Sparrow Press, 1984.

--, Tales of Ordinary Madness. San Francisco, City Lights Books, 1983.

--, The Day it Snowed in L.A. Santa Barbara, The Magnet Press, 1986.

--, The Days Run Away Like the Wild Horses Over the Hills. Santa Barbara, Black Sparrow Press, 1983.

--, The Most Beautiful Woman in Town and Other Stories. San Francisco, City Lights Books, 1983.

--, The Movie: 'Barfly'. Santa Barbara, Black Sparrow Press, 1987.

--, The Roominghouse Madrigals. Santa Barbara, Black Sparrow Press, 1988.

--, There's No Business. Santa Barbara, Black Sparrow Press, 1984.

--, War All the Time. Santa Barbara, Black Sparrow Press, 1984.

--, Women. Santa Barbara, Black Sparrow Press, 1983.

--, You Get So Alone At Times That It Just Makes Sense. Santa Barbara, Black Sparrow Press, 1986.

Carr, Jay, A Disarming Fairy tale View of Skid Row. The Boston Globe, 19 September 1987, Edition: Third.

--, Love is a Dog, Growing Up is Hard To Do. The Boston Globe, 10 June 1988.

--, Movie Madness' Marked by Confusion. The Boston Globe, 9 March 1984.

Cherkovski, Neeli, Hank: The Life of Charles Bukowski. New York, Random House, 1991.

Cismaru, Alfred, Marguerite Duras, New York, Twayne Publishers, 1971.

Clark, Tom, On the Trail of a Maverick Writer. The San Francisco Chronicle, 3 March 1991.

Cooney, Seamus, Ed. Charles Bukowski: Living On Luck: Select Letters 1960s-1970s. Santa Rosa, Black Sparrow Press, 1995.

--, Ed. Charles Bukowski: Screams from the Balcony: Select Letters 1960-1970. Santa Rosa, Black Sparrow Press, 1994.

Dretzka, Gary, Bukowski Reader Serves as a Literary Autobiography. The Chicago Tribune, 28 June 1993.

--, Los Angeles' Bard of Down and Out. The Chicago Tribune, 8 March 1991.

--, Skid Row Laureate Goes Respectable. The Chicago Tribune, 18 July 1989.

Duffy, Mike, Candid Documentary Chronicles Skid-Row Life. The Detroit Free Press, 4 December 1990, Edition: Final.

Duras, Marguerite, Agatha - Savannah Bay: 2 Plays By Marguerite Duras. Sausalito, The Post-Apollo Press, 1992.

--, Blue Eyes, Black Hair. New York, Pantheon Books, 1987.

--, Destroy She Said. New York, Grove Weinenfield, 1970.

--, Duras by Duras. San Fransisco, City Lights Books, 1987

--, India Song. New York, Grove Press, 1976.

--, The Lover. New York, Perennial Library, 1985.

--, The Malady of Death. New York, Grove Press, 1982.

--, The North China Lover. New York, The New Press, 1992.

--, Practicalities. New York, Grove Weidenfield, 1987.

--, The Ravishing of Lol Stein. New York, Pantheon Books, 1966.

--, The Sea Wall. New York, Farrar, Straus, &Giroux, 1952.

--, Two By Duras. Toronto, Coach House Press, 1982.

--, Summer Rain. New York, Collier Books. 1990.

--, The Vice-Consul. New York, Pantheon Books, 1966.

--, The War: A Memoir. New York, Pantheon Books, 1986.

Duras, Marguerite & Gauthier, Xaviere, Woman to Woman. Lincoln, University of Nebraska Press, 1987.

Duras, Marguerite, Yann Andrea Steiner. Charles Scribner's Son, New York, 1992.

Goldstein, Patrick, Gruff, Boozing Bukowski: A Media Darling PoetInspires Second Film. The San Francisco Chronicle, 17 July 1988.

Grossman, Ron, Marguerite Duras Makes No Sense. The Chicago Tribune, 27 May 1992.

Grumbach, Doris, Marguerite Duras Casts Experimental Lover. The Chicago Tribune, 9 June 1985

Harrison, Russell, Against the American Dream: Essays on Charles Bukowski. Santa Rosa, Black Sparrow Press, 1995.

Hemming, Sarah, Confessions Under Duras, The London Independent, 8 February 1995.

Howe, Desson, The Clinical Art of the Lover. The Washington Post, 13 November, 1992.

Huffhines, Kathy, Perverse Tale Spans Life Full of Disappointments. The Detroit Free Press, 24 March 1989.

Koch, Stephen, Mon Amour: Duras' Novel of Passion and Memory. The Washington Post, 21 July 1985.

Lacher, Irene, People: How Poetic - A Bukowski Wake. The Los Angeles Times, 24 March, 1994.

Locklin, Gerald, Charles Bukowski: A Sure Bet. Sudbury, Water Row Press, 1996.

Martin, John, Ed. Run With the Hunted: A Charles Bukowski Reader. New York, Harper Perennial, 1994.

Moody, Lori, Charles Bukowski Leaves a Controversial Legacy, The Chicago Tribune, 16 March 1994.

Munn, Lauren G., If Revenge is Duras' Aim, Then It Is Her Muse. The Chicago Tribune, 5 January 1993.

Murphy, Ray, The Antic Life of Charles Bukowski. The Boston Globe, 18 February 1991, Edition: Third.

Nicosia, Gerald, Down And Out in L.A. The Washington Post, 31 March 1991, Edition: Final.

Nundy, Julian, Book Review, The London Independent, 26 January 1992, Sunday Review Page.

Richmond, Steve, Spinning Off Bukowski. Northville, Sun Dog Press, 1996.

Rorem, Ned, Marguerite Duras: Lovers and Strangers. The Washington Post, 27 September 1987.

Schuster, Marilyn R., Marguerite Duras Revisited. New York, Twayne Publishers, 1993.

Schwartz, Stephen, Bukowski Liked His Life Rough and Raw. The San Fransisco Chronicle, 11 March 1994, Edition: Final.

Selous, Trista, The Other Woman: Feminism and Femininity in the Works of Marguerite Duras. New York, Yale University Press, 1988.

Vircondelet, Alain, Duras: A Biography. Normal, Dalkey Archive Press, 1994.

About the Author

Scott Shaw, Ph.D. is a prolific author, composer, filmmaker, journalist, and photographer.

Shaw's poetry and literary fiction first began to be published, in literary journals, in the late 1970s. He continued forward to have several works of poetry and literary fiction published in book form during the 1980s. By the mid 1980s, after having spent years traveled extensive throughout Asia, documenting obscure aspects of Asian culture in words and on film, his work on Social Science began to be published, as well. As the 1990s dawned, Shaw's writings began to be embraced in Spiritual and Martial Art circles. From this, he has authored numerous articles and a number of books on Zen Buddhism, Yoga, and the Martial Arts, published by large publishing houses.

Scott Shaw's *Books-In-Print* Overview:

About Peace: 108 Ways to Be at Peace When Things Are Out of Control, Published by Red Wheel/Weiser, United States

Advanced Taekwondo, Published by Tuttle Publications, United States

Alles op Zen tijd, Published by Mirananda Uitgeverd Publishing, The Netherlands

Čchi-kung pro začátečníky, Published by Pacvel Dobrovsky-BETA Publishing, The Czech Republic

Chi Kung for Beginners: Master the Flow of Chi for Good Health, Stress Reductions & Increased Energy, Published by Llewellyn Publications, United States

El Ki o la energia dinamica, Published by Selector Publishing, Mexico

El pequeño libro de la respiración: El Pranayama, de manera fácil, Published by Arkano Books, Spain

Hapkido: Korean Art of Self-Defense, Published by Tuttle Publications, United States

Hapkido, Published by Ehukc Publishing, Russia

Ki Process, Or Am Publishing, Israel

Qi Gong for Beginners, Published by Ehukc Publishing, Russia

157

Ki: Technici Eneggentice Coreene, Published by
Teora Publishing, Romania

Il Feluire Del Ki, Published by Edizioni Il Punto
D'Incontro, Italy

La Vita Secondo Lo Zen, Published by Gruppo
Editoriale Armenia, Italy

Lo Zen e la vita, Published by Gruppo Editoriale
Armenia, Italy

Mastering Health: The A to Z of Chi Kung, New
Age Books, India

Nirvana in a Nutshell: 157 Zen Meditations,
Published by Red Wheel/Weiser, United States

157 Zen Meditations AKA Nirvana in a Nutshell,
Published by Jaico Books, India

Nirvána dióhéjban 157 zen-meditáció, Published by
Lunarimprex Kiado, Hungary

Pránajáma dióhéjban, Published by Lunarimpex
Kiado, Hungary

Pranayama: A Respiracao Para Revitalizacao
Energetica, Published by Nova Era Publishing,
Brazil

Qi Gong for Beginners, Published by Ehukc
Publishing, Russia (ISBN: 5-8183-0966-5)

158

Samurai Zen, Published by Red Wheel/Weiser, United States

Simple Bliss: Nirvana Made Easy, Element Books, United Kingdom

Szamurai Zen, Published by Lunarimprex Kiado, Hungary

Taekwondo Basics, Published by Tuttle Publications, United States

Taekwondo Căn bản, Published by Nhân Văn Publishers, Vietnam

Taekwondo: 50 Essential Techniques, Published by AST, Russia

The Ki Process: Korean Secrets for Cultivating Dynamic Energy, Published by Red Wheel/Weiser, United States

The Little Book of Yoga Breathing: Pranayama Made Easy, Published by Red Wheel/Weiser, United States (ISBN: 1-57863-301-X)

The Little Book of Yoga Breathing: Pranayama Made Easy, Published by Jaico Books, India

The Tao of Self-Defense, Published by Red Wheel/Weiser, United States

The Warrior Is Silent: Martial Art and the Spiritual Path, Published by Inner Traditions International, United States

The Warrior is Silent, Published by Keopos Publishing, Greece

Zen-kapu a belső békességhez, Published by Lunarimprex Kiado, Hungary

Zen O'Clock: Time to Be, Published by Red Wheel/Weiser, United States

Zen Óra Mesterek és harci művészetek, Published by Lunarimprex Kiado, Hungary

www.ingramcontent.com/pod-product-compliance
Lightning Source LLC
Chambersburg PA
CBHW030418100426
42812CB00028B/3006/J